Motivated Minds

Building True Team Spirit – A Fireside Chat

Keith Trubshaw

ISBN: 978-1-66640-928-4 (paperback)
ISBN: 978-1-66640-929-1 (ebook)

Edited and Interior Layout by Penny Brucker (Upwork)

For permissions, inquiries, or bulk purchases, contact:
info@thelonelyseat.com

Author's Note

As you turn the pages of this book, you'll see that I've included a section called *Points to Ponder* at the end of each chapter. I make no apology for the lack of consistency in these sections in terms of their length and the way they are presented. Some are much longer than others. Some have bullet points, others do not. I sacrificed consistency in favour of being authentic and relevant to each individual chapter.

Too many books of this ilk become dry and difficult to read, not because of their content, but because of the statistics and evidence cited in support of what has been written. Where I was able, I have boxed off these statistics and citations so that they can be easily identified and skipped if you so wish.

Finally, I am something of a maverick. Many of the ideas and suggestions I present do not come from textbooks or management gurus; they are simply things that worked for me and are thus highly personal. You may disagree with sections (or even the entire book), but at least it will give you food for thought.

If you feel the need to contact me, I can be reached at: *info@thelonelyseat.com*

I hope you enjoy our fireside chat.

Contents

Introduction

Do you lead a team but find that you are struggling to build genuine team loyalty? Perhaps you sometimes feel like you're the only one who cares whether your team succeeds or fails. And no matter how hard you try, it feels lonely at the top.

What if there were ways to change that? Ways to create a team environment where everyone feels valued and ready to support one another, so you can end the isolation that comes with being the boss and restore the joy of coming to work.

Imagine leading a team that feels like family, where everyone is eager to contribute and help each other succeed. You feel a sense of relief, knowing you're not alone. You can take a vacation knowing that everything and everyone will be in good hands. The business will actually prosper while you're away. Think about what it will be like when you have built a team that pulls in the same direction and shares the same vision.

Imagine how the business would skyrocket to success if every single employee were an ambassador for it, singing its praises at every opportunity. And then, maybe best of all, imagine that promise of freedom that sang so loud when you started out, finally becoming a reality!

"The secret of getting ahead is getting started." Mark Twain's timeless wisdom reminds us that every journey, no matter how ambitious, begins with a single step. This book is that first step towards building something remarkable: a team that is not only successful but also engaged, motivated, and connected to a shared purpose.

This book takes the form of a fireside chat, offering insights, wisdom, and actionable strategies in a relaxed, conversational tone. Together, we'll explore the heart of what it means to build and lead a motivated, engaged, and high-performing team, not as a lecture, but as a meaningful dialogue.

There are two comfortable armchairs in front of the fire. Light a match, watch it crackle into life, sit back, and let the journey begin.

As a business leader, I'm willing to bet that you know the challenges of balancing operational goals, employee satisfaction, and long-term visions only too well. Maybe you often feel like some kind of circus performer, constantly spinning plates. Chances are that you've experienced moments of doubt, wondering if the effort you invest in your team is truly making a difference. Let me assure you: it is. But be warned; this is a double-edged sword. Breeding the wrong culture or closing your eyes to one that has gone sour will come home to bite you as sure as night follows day.

The culture you foster, the trust you build, the leadership you provide, and the inspiration you offer have a profound impact not just on your business outcomes but also on the lives of the people who work alongside you. Not only that, but it can also have a profound impact on how you are perceived by the world outside. If people like what they see, they will be far more likely to want to do business with you.

WHY THIS BOOK MATTERS

In today's fast-paced world, businesses face unprecedented challenges. Rapid technological advancements, not least in artificial intelligence, shifting market demands, and evolving workforce expectations make it clear that success is no longer just about profitability or efficiency. It's about people. The most resilient and innovative organisations are those that place employee engagement and motivation at the heart of their strategy. Gallup research indicates that highly engaged teams achieve 21% higher profitability and experience 41% lower absenteeism rates than their disengaged counterparts. If that's not a good enough reason to have this fireside chat, then I don't know what is. Clearly, engagement isn't just a "nice-to-have," it's a necessity.

But engagement is not a one-size-fits-all concept. Every team is unique and shaped by the personalities, values, and aspirations of its members. We are going to explore the nuances of building and sustaining a culture of engagement and come up with actionable insights tailored to the real-world challenges leaders face. Whether you're managing a small start-up or leading a global enterprise, the principles in this book will help you unlock your team's potential. This is a human game where everyone can win.

THE JOURNEY AHEAD

At the heart of this book is the belief that motivated minds drive true team success. Each chapter is a conversation; a fireside chat that explores key themes including trust, communication, recognition, and purpose. It's my sincere hope that as you turn the final pages, you'll have gained actionable insights into:

- Creating an engaged team by understanding the emotional and psychological drivers of motivation.

- Developing a leadership style that inspires trust and fosters collaboration.

- Navigating challenges with adaptability and resilience.

- Building a legacy of motivation and purpose that can endure well beyond your tenure.

We'll draw on proven research, real-world examples, and insights from business visionaries like Peter Drucker and Howard Schultz, as well as inspiration from luminaries like Maya Angelou and Helen Keller. These voices remind us that leadership is both an art and a science, requiring empathy, vision, and a commitment to continuous growth.

WHY ENGAGEMENT MATTERS NOW MORE THAN EVER

The world of work has undergone a seismic shift. Hybrid and remote work models have redefined how teams interact. Employees today seek more than just a wage or salary; they want meaningful work, opportunities for growth, and a sense of belonging (they probably always did, but little attention was paid to their needs). They need to be allowed to help create something they care about. As Margaret Wheatley said, "There is no power for change greater than a community discovering what it cares about." We have to rise to the challenge of creating workplaces that nurture this sense of community.

So, where is this fireside chat going to take us? Here are a few tasters for a start:

Stephen Covey said, "Trust is the glue of life." We will look at how to build the kind of trust that can be an unshakable foundation for team success. If trust is the glue of life, then communication is the rocket fuel. We'll discuss how to ensure every team member feels heard, valued, and, most of all, respected. We'll celebrate diversity and genuine inclusion as the bedrock of an innovation culture. While we are at it, we'll look at ways we might empower employees with autonomy and opportunities to grow that align with their own aspirations.

Perhaps you're thinking, "What if I do all this, and they leave?" My answer is this: "What if you don't, and they stay?"

This is where you should pause for thought and stare into the flames.

LEADERSHIP'S ROLE IN SHAPING CULTURE

Leadership is the capacity to translate vision into reality.

— Warren Bennis

Leadership is the cornerstone of engagement. A leader's ability to inspire, adapt, and connect sets the tone for the entire organisation. Your vision, when combined with your team's collective talents and motivations, becomes the engine of transformation.

This fireside chat isn't about achieving perfection; it's about progress. It's about taking intentional steps to create an environment where every team member feels empowered to contribute their best. It's about understanding that the challenges, growth, and collaboration along the journey are just as important as the destination. Indeed, without that journey, the destination will be forever out of reach.

A CALL TO ACTION

As you warm your toes near this crackling fire, I encourage you to reflect on your leadership journey. Consider the legacy you want to leave. Think about the moments when your team has thrived and the lessons learned from setbacks. Remember, the path to true team success begins with motivated minds, including yours.

I make no apology for repeating Mark Twain's words, "The secret of getting ahead is getting started." Let's begin this journey together, building teams that are not only high-performing but also deeply connected to a shared vision. Together, we can create a workplace where engagement isn't just an ideal but a lived reality.

So, take that first step. The best is yet to come.

Chapter 1

The Power of a Motivated Mind

UNDERSTANDING EMPLOYEE ENGAGEMENT

When people are financially invested, they want a return. When people are emotionally invested, they want to contribute.

— Simon Sinek

Here we are, the fire's crackling softly in the hearth. Let's share a moment to reflect. You're carrying a lot on your shoulders, and sometimes, it feels like you're tackling everything alone. There is something that could transform not only your business but also how you feel about running it. It consists of just two words that, when you first hear them, you'll probably roll your eyes and say, " I'm wasting your time. The words are "employee engagement". Hear me out.

Employee engagement isn't just a buzzword; it's the heartbeat of any thriving business. Think of it as the force that turns individual employees into a team that's more than the sum of its parts. When people are engaged, they don't just complete tasks; they bring energy, creativity, and commitment to the mission. They feel connected to something bigger than themselves, and that connection fuels innovation and resilience. You can't tell me that wouldn't be nice!

Research conducted by Gallup found that organisations with highly engaged employees have 21% higher profitability compared to those with low engagement *(Gallup, 2017)*.

This isn't just about numbers; it's about creating a culture where people are happy, even excited to come to work every day. It's not just me saying this; consider companies like Southwest Airlines, whose focus on employee satisfaction has led to decades of customer loyalty and consistent profitability.

Henry Ford famously said, "Coming together is a beginning, staying together is progress, and working together is success." Engagement is the chemistry that turns a group of individuals into a united, thriving team. It all starts with a simple but profound idea: engagement begins with you. It's about creating an environment where your team feels valued, heard, and empowered to contribute. Imagine a workplace where employees don't just clock in and out; they show up because they're invested in your vision. This kind of culture doesn't happen by accident. It takes intention, but the rewards are immense.

At its core, engagement is about emotional commitment. This goes far beyond job satisfaction or meeting KPIs; it's about building a culture where people care deeply about their work and the success of the whole organisation. When your team is emotionally connected, they go the extra mile, collaborate effortlessly, and feel pride in being part of something meaningful. Andrew Carnegie aptly put it: "Teamwork is the fuel that allows common people to attain uncommon results." I'd put it this way: "Collaborative energy drives extraordinary outcomes."

Think of engagement not just as an end in itself but as a living, breathing force. Celebrate small victories. Each is a brushstroke within the canvas you are collectively trying to paint. Applaud team members when they act with care and intention. That applause doesn't have to be sung from the highest treetop. Such things might embarrass the recipient. Sometimes, it's better to take the opportunity to do it quietly, one-on-one. You'll be astounded at the results.

Starting today, see engagement as far more than just a foundation. It is a true catalyst for transcending the mediocrity that can result from an organisation being pulled in too many directions. Think about what would happen if you sought not only loyalty but creativity from every employee. Chances are, it will make them feel their job is meaningful. They'd know they are contributing to something much larger than themselves.

We should strive to create an environment where employees feel empowered. Just imagine that the time and encouragement you give them, and they give to each other, lets them begin to feel unstoppable. Encourage everyone to set out what their dream day would look like. Encourage them to envision their most impactful role. Then work with them to explore ways of making that vision a reality. Even if it turns out to be pie in the sky, you will have involved them in the process, and the level of understanding between you will rise to a whole new level.

EFFECTIVE HIRING

Hiring plays a crucial role here. When you bring people into your team who resonate with your values and vision, you lay the foundation for something extraordinary. Picture the kind of energy that builds when every team member shares a common purpose.

Okay, it's generally accepted wisdom that we should seek alignment through open dialogue and transparency, but hiring isn't just about alignment; it's about evolution. Each new hire redefines your culture. They can move you backwards, keep you still, or move you forward. Don't shy away from disruptors who could challenge the norm and stretch the team. One of my favourite sayings has always been "Employ Giants."

To be successful, hiring is like producing a fine wine. The process shouldn't be rushed. Apple, one of the most successful companies on the planet, makes a point of going slowly. Technical ability is a given, but they go far beyond it. They look for those who are most likely to fit in, to help move the company forward, if only in a small way. They look for the ability and preparedness to work across departments, and in that regard, see the big picture instead of seeking the comfort of being in a single silo.

COMMUNICATION

Communication is both the glue that holds everything together and the rocket fuel that can take things to new heights. How often do you create space for open dialogue with your team? I'm not just talking about formal meetings with an agenda. In my experience, such meetings often stifle people's willingness to be open and honest about what they really feel; it's better to stay quiet and not upset the apple cart! Regular, informal, off-the-cuff conversations, where employees feel safe sharing their ideas and feedback, are the bedrock of trust.

A study by Harvard Business Review found that leaders who foster a culture of transparency and regular feedback see a 60% improvement in employee satisfaction *(Harvard Business Review, 2016)*.

When you listen—truly listen—and that means listen with both ears, not distracted by something else that's just flashed up on your screen, you'll be amazed at what your team can contribute. Their insights, creativity, and even their critiques will become some of your most valuable resources.

LEADERSHIP

Let's talk about leadership. When was the last time you invested in your own growth as a leader? Leadership isn't about having all the answers; it's about inspiring others to believe in themselves and the work you're doing together.

Howard Schultz, the former CEO of Starbucks, once said, "When you're surrounded by people who share a passionate commitment around a common purpose, anything is possible" *(Schultz, 2011)*.

Show your team that you're committed to growing and learning alongside them, and watch as they mirror that dedication. Together, you'll build a culture of resilience, innovation, and engagement that will take your business to heights you would never have thought possible.

MOTIVATION

How many books have been written about this single word? Countless! What a topic, what a question! What is motivation? How do we achieve it in ourselves and others?

Let's look at the carrot and the stick analogy[1]. The stick doesn't work. People leave as soon as they can, or else work in fear, in which case any chance of them being creative or loyal when your back is turned jumps out of the window. The carrot works for longer than the stick, but once again, if people are just working for the money, in the end, they will leave as soon as a better offer comes their way. True motivation comes from the heart. People buy into your why, and it becomes a common why. And here's the thing: they will only do that when they instinctively know that they are contributing. It has to be inside them at an emotional level.

Motivation and engagement go hand in hand. When your team is motivated, their engagement skyrockets; they don't just show up; they lean in. They become the kind of team that can tackle any challenge and turn obstacles into opportunities. Let me ask you this: what kind of legacy do you want to leave as a leader? What if the key to unlocking your team's potential was simply showing them how much they matter?

TRUST

And then there's trust. Trust is another cornerstone of motivation. When your team feels supported and efforts are recognised, it builds a culture of mutual respect. This trust creates a safe space where people aren't afraid to share ideas, take risks, and innovate. As their leader, you have the chance to nurture this trust every day. You should develop a nose for those opportunities. Don't let them pass you by because you have "more important" things to do.

Trust isn't just about safety and reliance; it's the soil where dreams grow. Ask yourself, "How much do I trust them?" If the answer is "I don't", then sit down

---

[1] My editor tells me that I should explain the "carrot and stick" analogy. It comes from the idea of moving a donkey by either dangling a carrot as a reward or hitting it with a stick as punishment. The stick creates fear and drives people away, while the carrot — like a paycheck or bonus — only works temporarily. True motivation lasts when people connect to your "why" and feel their contributions truly matter."

with yourself and ask why you don't. Be honest. Could it be that they failed in the past? That begs another question: "Did they fail because you pushed them beyond their capability? Could it be that you have never trusted them?" In which case, assign them to a task, let them know it's important, and make sure that they know it's okay to ask for help. Give them a chance to shine!

Now, let's dive into the heart of what motivation can do for your team. Imagine your team as a group of mountaineers, each person tackling a rugged trail. Some days, the path is steep and rocky, and the summit seems impossibly far away. Motivation is the force that keeps everyone moving upward, even when the climb is tough. But remember that as the leader, you set the pace.

Motivation fuels your team's ability to push boundaries and achieve remarkable things. When people feel inspired, they don't just meet expectations, they exceed them. They collaborate more freely, solve problems more creatively, and show up for one another. As the leader, it's your job to create an environment where this kind of motivation can flourish.

> Google's famous "20% time" policy, where employees are encouraged to dedicate 20% of their time to passion projects, has led to innovations like Gmail and Google Maps, proving that when employees are given freedom and motivation, their creativity knows no bounds *(Bock, 2015)*.

Maybe your organisation doesn't have the resources to allow people such freedom. Well, here's the news, most will take it anyhow, whether it's in the form of extended visits to the restroom or indulging in office chat about last night's TV. Why not make a point of steering that time into projects of their own choosing? Perhaps they will come up with something special, perhaps they won't. But either way, they will know that they are being allowed to express themselves.

In my experience, if someone felt they were onto something special, I almost always encouraged them by allowing them more time to pursue it and see where it led. You may think that caused resentment amongst other team members. It didn't. On the contrary, because of the non-combative team spirit we had built, they applauded what was being done and often used their own development freedom to help with their workmate's project. They understood how it would benefit everyone, themselves included.

Think about what drives your team. Are they clear on the vision? Have they bought into your why? Do they see how their contributions fit into the bigger picture? When people understand their purpose and feel their work matters, it ignites something powerful within them. They feel a sense of pride and ownership that transforms how they approach their roles. One of my favourite examples of this kind of thing in action is the story of when President Kennedy visited the NASA moon landing project. He needed to use the restroom and spoke to the janitor there. When the president asked him what he did there at NASA, the janitor proudly replied that he was helping put a man on the moon!

Start each day with this question: "What can I do to make someone on my team feel that they are seen and heard?"

Ask yourself right now, "What's the one thing I could do to ignite joy and freedom in what I do so that it becomes infectious throughout the whole business?"

Let's build something incredible. It starts here, with this conversation by the fire, igniting another kind of fire in your heart to make things better. For your team, for your business, and for yourself.

POINTS TO PONDER

Putting Employee Engagement Insights into Radical Practice

Employee engagement is not a checklist item or a one-time initiative; it's the lifeblood of thriving businesses. We have laid the foundation for understanding engagement and its transformative power. Let's explore how a forward-thinking leader can break conventional moulds and innovate their approach to building an engaged and motivated team. I'm going to suggest some unorthodox yet actionable strategies to translate what we've discussed into groundbreaking results. You may like them, you may not. You might discard some, you might embrace others. Either way, I hope you will find a few gems that can help you move towards a more engaged, supportive, and happier team.

Start With Radical Self-Honesty

The journey toward revolutionising your team begins with a brutally honest self-assessment. As the leader, you set the tone. Do you truly embody the values you preach? And here is the sixty-four-thousand-dollar question: Would you thrive as an employee in your organisation? Sit with these questions until they make you uncomfortable, because discomfort is the precursor to growth.

Host an anonymous feedback session. But here's the twist: let your team evaluate you first. Provide a platform where employees can share what inspires them about your leadership and what leaves them uninspired. Commit to listening with an open heart, resisting defensiveness, and acting on the feedback. This act of vulnerability establishes trust and demonstrates your commitment to growth alongside your team.

Turn Meetings Into Micro-Missions

Traditional meetings are often seen as necessary evils. To engage your team, flip the script on how meetings function. Every meeting should have one audacious goal: to solve a real, pressing issue that affects the team's daily experience. Replace stale agendas with "micro-missions" – short, focused tasks designed to resolve specific pain points.

For example, if engagement feels low because employees are disconnected from the company's purpose, use a meeting to co-create a mission statement. Pose the question, "What do we want to stand for as a team?" and let everyone contribute. Facilitate with curiosity, ensuring every voice is heard. The act of collectively shaping the mission will inject purpose and energy into your team.

Elevate Recognition Beyond Ritual

Recognition programs are often formulaic, but genuine recognition should be transformative, not transactional. Break away from the standard employee of the month framework and create a culture of spontaneous, specific, and story-driven praise.

Imagine a system where every team member keeps a "Recognition Journal," a physical or digital space to note when a colleague does something remarkable. Once a week, during a casual huddle, individuals share these moments aloud. Hearing peers articulate specific examples of their contributions fosters pride and camaraderie, embedding recognition into the team's fabric. But a word of warning: don't force this issue. It's important that these commendations aren't forced – just devised for the sake of having to come up with something, anything! That would rob the system of its validity faster than a phone thief on a moped. When they arise, record them and celebrate them. Look for the good.

Make Autonomy Your Competitive Edge

Micromanagement is the silent killer of engagement. Flip the traditional hierarchy by becoming a resource, not a boss. Empower your team to make decisions by implementing a framework called "Autonomy Zones." Define clear boundaries where employees have full decision-making authority. Whether it's redesigning the workspace, choosing new tools, or spearheading client strategies, give them room to experiment.

To ensure autonomy doesn't spiral into chaos, create a culture of "post-mortems." This is a team exercise in which you envision why a decision could fail and collaboratively address risks before moving forward. This approach fosters ownership while providing a safety net for bold ideas.

Build Rituals of Belonging

Engagement thrives on connection. Instead of generic team-building exercises, create unique rituals that resonate with your team's identity. Some might suggest implementing a monthly "Gratitude Shift," where each team member writes down one thing they're grateful for about a colleague and delivers it in person or through a meaningful note. The theory is that such rituals cultivate a culture of appreciation and humanise workplace interactions. But once again, a word of warning: if you take this path, don't force the issue. I confess that even though I'm mentioning it as something you may wish to consider, in general, I'm not a fan of formalised events such as this. Indeed, if there are so many ritualised gratitude parties, they will rob genuine expressions of appreciation of their value. It doesn't have to be formal or complicated. If someone wants to express gratitude, create a platform that encourages them to do so.

Something else you might want to think about is hosting "Fail Forwards Fridays." Once a month, invite team members to share a mistake they made, what they learned, and how they moved forward. This practice not only normalises failure but also strengthens trust and resilience. Done without formality, it can introduce laughter in a nurturing environment, an ultimate team builder if ever there was one.

Redefine Success Metrics

To truly embed engagement into your team's DNA, reimagine what success looks like. Traditional metrics, such as profitability and efficiency, are essential, but they're incomplete. Incorporate metrics that reflect emotional and psychological engagement.

For instance:

- **Belonging Index**: Use surveys or qualitative interviews to measure employee connection to their peers and the organisation's mission.

- **Resilience Score**: Track how employees rebound from challenges, both individually and collectively. Celebrate stories of perseverance.

- **Creative Impact**: Evaluate the frequency and quality of new ideas generated by the team, even those that don't lead to immediate implementation.

These unconventional metrics will allow you to pivot from short-term gains to long-term engagement and innovation.

Embrace a Legacy Mindset

Leading a team isn't about being the hero; it's about creating a culture that thrives without you. Ask yourself, "If I left tomorrow, what would endure?"

Begin cultivating successors who embody your values and can advance the mission. Mentor them not just in skills but in mindset and emotional intelligence.

Take your legacy-building further by involving the team in defining what your organisation should stand for in the years to come. Encourage employees to imagine what future team members will say about the culture they helped shape. Don't just do this as a one-off exercise. Revisit it regularly. In that way, you can reinforce the idea that engagement is a shared responsibility and a lasting endeavour.

Create a Ripple Effect

Radical engagement doesn't stop with your team. Its influence should extend to clients, partners, and the broader community. Design initiatives where your team's engagement inspires external stakeholders. For example, adopt a "Give Back Day" where employees volunteer together for causes they care about. This not only reinforces purpose but also positions your organisation as a force for good.

Another bold move is to invite clients or customers to co-create solutions with your team. By breaking down silos and extending the spirit of collaboration, you deepen engagement both internally and externally. A client who has played a role in helping your organisation develop, especially in a way that benefits them, is unlikely to be tempted to go elsewhere.

To put this chapter's principles into practice is to lead with audacity by challenging norms, embracing vulnerability, and prioritising human connection over conventional KPIs. Dare to reimagine what an engaged workplace looks like. Cultivate a culture so vibrant, so genuine that it becomes your competitive edge.

True engagement doesn't just drive business outcomes; it transforms lives. By daring to be radically different, you can create a legacy that extends beyond profit margins, a legacy of impact, inspiration, and enduring human connection.

Chapter 2

Building a True Team

DEFINING TEAM DYNAMICS

Picture this: you and your team aren't just a group of individuals working in silos, but a dynamic, interconnected force, each part complementing the other. That's the magic of strong team dynamics, and it's achievable when we focus on the relationships and interactions that shape collaboration and morale. But I know it's easier said than done, right? Let's explore this together.

Strong team dynamics start with trust. Imagine your team as a circle, where each person feels safe enough to share their ideas and take risks without fear of judgment. Trust is the foundation of this circle, and it begins with you.

> Research from PwC highlights that 74% of employees in high-trust organisations feel less stressed and are 50% more productive *(PwC, 2018)*. For example, Google fosters trust through its 'Project Aristotle', which revealed that psychological safety, where team members feel comfortable being vulnerable, is the most important factor in team success *(Bock, 2015)*.

But trust alone isn't enough. Communication is the ultimate glue that holds your team together. Think about how often you pause to really hear your employees, not just their words but the meaning behind them. Open channels of communication, whether through regular check-ins, brainstorming sessions, or casual conversations, are the lifeblood of effective team dynamics. When people feel heard, they feel valued.

> A Harvard Business Review study found that organisations with open communication practices see a 47% increase in collaboration and efficiency *(Harvard Business Review, 2016).*

And let's not forget individuality. Every person on your team brings a unique set of strengths, experiences, and perspectives. When did you last take the time to uncover those? Encouraging your team to collaborate based on their strengths doesn't just build morale; it creates strong bonds. Allowing individuals the freedom to play to their strengths is one of the keys to happiness and fulfilment in the workplace. It doesn't take a rocket scientist to figure out that a happy team leads to greater productivity and significantly lower staff turnover.

As we sit here and talk about building your team, let me assure you, it doesn't have to be perfect. What matters is your willingness to intentionally foster these dynamics. Start small. One open conversation. One moment of recognition. Watch how these ripples turn into waves of trust and connection.

CREATING A SHARED VISION

Close your eyes and imagine your team not working for you but *with* you. Imagine them as co-creators of a vision that excites and inspires. That's the power of a shared vision. It transforms your business from a job into a mission.

Creating a shared vision starts with clarity. What's your "why"? Why does your business exist, and where do you see it going? Share this openly with your team, not just the polished version but the real, heartfelt one. Let them see your passion and hear your hopes. When people understand the "why," they're far more likely to connect with the "how."

But a shared vision isn't just about you. It's about bringing your team into the conversation. Ask them about their aspirations and how they see themselves contributing to the bigger picture. These conversations are opportunities to align individual goals with the collective mission. When your employees feel like stakeholders in the vision, they invest more of themselves in achieving it.

It's all very well showing your team your vision and expecting them to buy into it lock, stock, and barrel. This is the real world. You have to give a little, too. A tiny shift from you to accommodate their aspirations can mean that everyone wins. Wouldn't you prefer reaching your goal just one per cent off course from your original intention as opposed to floundering well short of the mark because you couldn't take people along with you?

Then comes the storytelling. Don't just lay out a plan, paint a picture. Use stories to illustrate what success looks like and how their roles play a part in getting there. Stories stick with us. They inspire action in ways that bullet points never can.

But now I hear you ask, "What kind of stories? I'm not a storyteller!" I'm here to tell you that you are—maybe not an expert—but nevertheless, you are.. Everyone is a storyteller. But let's get back to your question, "What kind of stories?" Think of painting a picture in time. The picture isn't static; it's more like a movie screen. We start by describing the way things used to be in the good old days (or maybe not), if you like. Then, describe how you felt over time as things changed and evolved. Remember, the idea is not to bore them with a list of facts, but to draw people into the story so that they can empathise with the way you felt at the time. From this feeling of empathy, they will begin to understand and, more importantly, buy into what you are trying to achieve. This isn't about money; it's about how you will feel and how THEY will feel when they join you on the journey.

A shared vision is alive. It grows and evolves as your business does. Keep revisiting it, celebrating progress, and recalibrating it as a team when needed. By doing so, you create a dynamic and enthusiastic team ready to tackle any challenge with a unified sense of purpose.

CULTIVATING A CULTURE OF COLLABORATION

Let's talk about collaboration, not just working together but truly building something together. Imagine your team as an orchestra, each instrument playing its part to create harmony. That's the essence of collaboration, and it's where businesses find their stride. From where you are, you see all the parts begin to work smoothly together, but here's the thing: if you get it right, everyone else can see and appreciate that too.

Collaboration begins with the right environment. Are you creating spaces where your team feels safe to speak up, share ideas, and even disagree? Disagreements, when handled respectfully, can spark creativity and innovation.

> Pixar's Braintrust meetings, where directors receive candid feedback on their projects, are a prime example of collaboration in action. This approach has led to some of the studio's most iconic films, from *Toy Story* to *Inside Out (Catmull, 2014)*.

That example is well established in the public domain, but let me give you a very personal one. I attended a boys' school. Every lunchtime, come rain or shine, we played football. It didn't matter whether the ball was a good one, a burst one, a big one, or a small one. We played football. Was I the best player? No! Was I the worst player? No! We were all pretty okay, whatever that means. There was another lad called Dev. One day, we were on the same team, but we had fallen out over something stupid, like not passing the ball. It descended into a full-blown argument. Both of us said what we thought, and then it ended as quickly as it had begun. Here's the thing: following that (let's call it very frank) conversation, we could have ignored each other when it came to working on the same team, but the opposite occurred. That frank conversation led to us playing the best football we had ever played.

Then there's the importance of recognition. Collaboration thrives when people feel their contributions are seen and valued. A simple thank-you or acknowledgement during a meeting can go a long way. When your team sees that their efforts matter, they'll go above and beyond for each other. But here's the thing: a "well done" delivered directly from the boss is a great tool for lifting someone's morale, but it pales into insignificance when it's followed up by someone else telling that team member something like, "The boss was singing your praises." That team member knows that the direct congratulation wasn't just a throw-away comment... they had been noticed!

It's also about tools and processes. Do you have systems in place that help make collaboration seamless? Whether it's project management software like Asana or team chat platforms like Slack, the right tools can make all the difference. But remember, tools are just the enablers—it's the culture you build that makes collaboration stick.

As we sit here, I hope your cogs are turning. You're imagining what a truly collaborative team could look like for your business. And you're right to dream big. Collaboration isn't just a nice-to-have. It's the engine that drives creativity, resilience, and growth. You'll be amazed at where it can take you.

POINTS TO PONDER

Hold a "Trust Check-In"

Trust isn't declared, it's felt. Choose a moment this week to ask your team a single powerful question: "Do you feel safe to speak your mind here?" You don't need a formal survey, just a space where honest answers are welcome. Your response isn't to defend or explain, but to listen —really listen. Trust grows in silence as much as in speech.

Start a Strengths Discovery Exercise

Book a 45-minute session titled: "What Do I Bring to the Table?" Ask each team member to share what they believe their greatest strength is, and then invite their peers to add their observations. You'll be amazed at how affirming and illuminating this is. Don't overdo it; limit the session to just one or two people per session. Let it breathe.

Run a "Vision Walk" Conversation.

Instead of sitting around a boardroom table, invite one or two team members for a walk (real or virtual) and talk them through your "why." Then ask them about theirs. What gets them out of bed? Where do they want to go? Capture themes and look for where personal and business visions naturally align. That's where momentum lives.

Introduce "Conflict With Care" Guidelines

Put together a list called "How We Disagree" and have the team co-create it. This becomes a live, working agreement on how to handle tensions. Normalise disagreement as a creative act, not something to fear. Like that football game, you may play your best after an honest clash.

Set a "Whispers of Praise" Challenge

Try this: for every piece of direct praise you give, challenge yourself to make sure someone else repeats it to the team member within a day. You'll build a culture of reinforcement where appreciation echoes, not just lands and vanishes.

Audit Your Collaboration Toolkit

Take a 10-minute solo check-in: *Do our tools help us or hinder us?* Write down what's being used: Slack, Zoom, Google Docs, whiteboards, and meetings. Then ask your team: "What do we love, what do we loathe, and what's missing?" The goal isn't more tools, but fewer that actually serve your team.

Visualise Your Team as a Circle, Not a Pyramid

Take a sheet of paper and draw a representation of your team. Use a circle for the template rather than a hierarchy. Who's in it? Who's on the edge? Who's not even on the page but should be? Now ask yourself: "What's one thing I could do this week to bring someone closer to the centre?"

Each of these actions is deliberately small. Not because your ambitions are small, but because trust, collaboration, and vision are built through consistent moments, not grand gestures. Think of them like striking matches. Enough of them together, and suddenly, you have a fire worth gathering around.

Chapter 3

Hiring for Team Culture Fit

IDENTIFYING CORE VALUES

Let's talk about your team's foundation. Core values aren't just words on a wall or in a mission statement; they're the guiding principles that shape your business's culture and every decision you make. Think of them as the roots of a tree: unseen but vital, grounding everything above. So, what are your core values, and are they reflected in the team you've built?

Culture is not a mission statement. It's the pulse of your organisation, how it feels, sounds, and moves. To hire for culture fit, you have to articulate what your culture truly is. Defining core values starts with reflection. What do you stand for? What principles have guided your business through its successes and challenges? Take the time to sit with these questions. Don't stop there; bring your team into the conversation.

> For example, when Zappos (a success story if ever there was one) was defining its core values, the leadership team involved employees at all levels, ensuring the final list reflected the company's collective identity (*Hsieh, 2010*).

By inviting your employees to share what they value, you're not just defining core values; you're embedding them into the heart of your culture.

Once you've defined these values, bring them to life. They need to be a living, breathing part of your business. From how you hire to how you celebrate achievements, your core values should be visible and tangible. For instance, if one of your values is integrity, show it by fostering transparency in communication. If innovation is a value, encourage creativity and reward fresh ideas. When your team sees your values in action, they'll embody them naturally.

Core values are the lens through which you can and should evaluate every decision.

As Howard Schultz, former CEO of Starbucks, once said, "If people believe they share values with a company, they will stay loyal to the brand" (*Schultz, 2011*).

By aligning your business decisions with your core values, you create a culture where employees feel connected and committed. Connected and committed employees can be the greatest sales team you could ever have. In a word, they will be ambassadors. There can be no better sales force than every employee singing the company's praises at every opportunity and meaning every word they say.

CRAFTING EFFECTIVE JOB DESCRIPTIONS

Imagine how good it would be if the next person you hire not only meets the job requirements but also elevates your team. They align with your values, thrive in your culture, and bring fresh energy to the business. It all starts with the job description.

A good job description does more than list tasks; it tells a story. It paints a picture of what it's like to be part of your team, to work toward the goals you've set, and to contribute to a vision that matters.

Take the example of HubSpot, which includes its culture code in every job listing. This transparency ensures candidates understand not just the role but the environment they'll be joining (*HubSpot, 2019*).

Start with clarity. Outline the key responsibilities of the role, but don't stop there. Share how this role fits into the bigger picture. What impact will this person have on your business? Bring in your values. Use language that reflects the culture you've worked so hard to create. Reimagine job descriptions as compelling narratives of purpose. If collaboration is one of your values, make it clear that teamwork is an essential part of the role. Yes, I know, everyone says that teamwork is essential, but how many would-be employers actually mean it? How many embrace the idea in what they do, not just what they say?

Transparency is equally important. Be upfront about expectations and opportunities for growth. Candidates appreciate honesty, and it sets the stage for a strong, trusting relationship from the start. Remember, you're not just hiring someone to fill a position; you're inviting them to be part of your journey. How do we demonstrate honesty? Here's a thought: As well as lauding the strengths of the company, how about admitting some of its shortcomings, areas that you admit could be improved?

Crafting job descriptions with intention not only attracts the right talent but also sets the tone for the culture you're building. Let's make every hire count.

INTERVIEW TECHNIQUES FOR CULTURE FIT

Now, picture this: you're in the middle of an interview, and something clicks. The person across from you isn't just qualified, they're aligned. They get your vision. They fit your culture. How do you make sure every interview leads to moments like this?

Start with behavioural questions that uncover a candidate's values and approach. For example, ask about a time they worked through a challenge or collaborated with a team to solve a problem. Let them know it's okay to include times when they failed and fell on their metaphorical backside. Listen for responses that reflect adaptability, resilience, and alignment with your core values. Most of all, listen for responses that demonstrate caring, honesty (no one is perfect), and vulnerability.

Involve your team in the process. Let candidates meet the people they'll be working with. This not only gives your team a say in the decision but also shows candidates what your culture feels like. It's a two-way street where you're evaluating them, and they're evaluating you.

Consider adding practical elements to your interviews. Simulate real work scenarios or ask candidates to brainstorm solutions to a hypothetical challenge. If it's practical, invite them in for a play day where they will get to know the organisation and you will get to know them. These exercises reveal how they think, collaborate, and contribute under pressure and in a meaningful context. On one occasion, we were holding a senior managers' meeting on a day when two pre-university interns were to start with my company. We invited them to sit in on the meeting, and the team involved them in the discussion. At first, they seemed a little punch-drunk by the kind of information coming their way, but as the meeting went on, they relaxed and contributed from a perspective we would otherwise not have considered. Being part of that all-day meeting helped them bloom into an intricate part of the business. They bought into the culture… it was wonderful to see. All at the cost of two extra lunch places!

Okay, so we've discussed the standard things we should do, but what about something that I call mouldability? If you have two candidates, one provides excellent examples of how they coped with situations similar to those they're likely to encounter if they get the job. They're vastly experienced and would clearly be a valuable asset. The other can't (or maybe doesn't want to) recall everything in the same detail, but instinctively, you like them. Your head says to choose the better qualified, and your head would probably be right. BUT, and it's a big but, the first candidate may be set in their ways, and their ways of doing things may smack of "it has to be done my way". However, the second candidate might just be more flexible and, as a consequence, more mouldable to the company's values.

It may be worthwhile to have them sit in on meetings held by people in roles more senior to the job they are looking for.

Be transparent about your values and expectations. Share your vision for the team and the role they'd play in achieving it. When candidates know what you stand for, they can self-assess whether they're a good fit. The result? You'll attract people who are not only capable but also genuinely excited to be part of your journey. It's the ones who are excited and stay excited who can be the best fit.

Interviewing for culture fit isn't just about filling roles; it's about building a team that thrives together. As we sit here discussing your next steps, let's make every hire a step toward the business you dream of leading.

POINTS TO PONDER

We've been looking at the art and science of hiring for culture fit, presenting it as the linchpin of organisational success. How do we elevate these principles into actionable strategies? How might we build a hiring process that doesn't just find employees but discovers champions?

Clarify Your Core Values With the Team

Engage in formal and informal discussions with your whole team. Ask three questions:

- What do you think our company stands for?

- What makes us different?

- What do you personally value most in the way we work together?

Collect answers on a whiteboard or shared doc. The aim is to create a living, breathing document. Highlight recurring themes. Chances are, they're your living values, not the ones dreamt up in a strategy workshop, and definitely the ones your hiring process must reflect.

Audit Your Current Team for Value Alignment

I know this sounds archaic, but bear with me on this. Take a sheet of paper and draw two columns. On the left, list your core values. On the right, write the names of team members. Now ask yourself quietly: "Who actively reflects each value? Who struggles with them?" This isn't about judgment, it's about awareness. Do your next hires need to reinforce strengths or fill gaps?

Job Descriptions That Tell a Story

Traditional job descriptions are static lists of tasks and qualifications. Transform them into narratives that reflect your culture and inspire the right candidates to envision themselves in the role. Instead of requirements, use headers like "What Your Day Might Look Like" or "How You'll Make an Impact." A candidate who can see from the outset how the job they are seeking fits into the organisation as a whole and understands how important it is to everyone's success, no matter how lowly the post, is a candidate who will be more enthusiastic about taking the job, and, if that sense of appreciation remains, be far more likely to stay. Before offering a role, have a final, non-technical chat. You or a team lead might say: "Here's what we're really like when no one's looking. How does that sit with you?" This honesty opens space for the candidate to ask real questions, too. Trust flows both ways. Describe some of the cross-functional sessions they'll be asked to participate in. Use stories of past sessions and how everyone's opinion is valued. These stories not only attract candidates aligned with your values but also deter those who wouldn't thrive in your environment.

Invite your final-round candidate to sit in on part of a real meeting or join a lunch-and-learn. Let them observe your team in action or even contribute, if appropriate. This small gesture demystifies your culture and helps both sides make a clearer, mutual choice.

Reflect on 'Mouldability' After Every Interview

After the formalities, take a quiet 5 minutes to ask yourself:

- *Can I see this person growing here?*

- *Are they excited about who we are, not just what we do?*

- *Could this person become a cornerstone of the culture we're building?*

I know this is anything but scientific, but sometimes, your gut knows. And when you temper instinct with reflection, you can find real gold.

Embrace Values-Based Screening

Resumes and technical interviews only tell part of the story. To truly hire for culture fit, incorporate values-based screening into your hiring process. Develop a questionnaire or exercise that probes candidates' alignment with your core values. Simply put, take the time to try to get to know them! Ask them about past experiences, not necessarily the technical successes and failures, but how they felt about them. This isn't an exercise for monotonous form-filling. In my experience, such things only produce what the candidate thinks we want to hear. The best results are through simple, relaxed conversations. Here's a thought in that regard: The interview might be conducted from opposite sides of your desk. Suggest that you adjourn for a coffee break. Go to the kitchen or canteen, a different environment, and do your best to make them feel at ease, that this is a conversation between equals. If that is something you're uncomfortable with, introduce the candidate to someone else, let them go off somewhere, and come back later. In the next section, I'll talk about the hiring process being something that the whole team should participate in. What I'm suggesting here can be part of that exercise.

Let the Team Lead the Interview

Cultural alignment isn't just about pleasing the hiring manager; it's about fitting into the team's ecosystem. After the initial screening, hand the reins to the team they'll work with. Create a "Day in the Life" interview, where candidates spend time shadowing, brainstorming, or problem-solving with the team. Encourage the team to evaluate candidates not just on technical prowess but on energy, communication style, and adaptability. This approach provides candidates with a firsthand experience of the workplace culture and empowers your team to take ownership of their hiring decisions.

Evaluate for Mouldability, Not Perfection

Hiring for culture fit doesn't mean hiring clones. Diversity of thought, background, and experience is critical to innovation. Focus on candidates' "mouldability" to learn about their willingness and ability to adapt, learn, and grow within your culture. Pay attention to enthusiasm, humility, and self-awareness. A candidate who demonstrates curiosity and adaptability will enrich your culture in ways that a perfect technical fit never could.

Make Onboarding a Cultural Immersion

The hiring process doesn't end when the offer is signed. Onboarding is your chance to solidify cultural alignment. Design an onboarding experience that immerses new hires in your values and norms. Consider pairing them with a "Culture Buddy" who is a seasoned team member who can answer questions, provide context, and model the organisation's values in action. But take care here, the choice of culture buddy is critical if the process is to succeed.

Lead by Example

Culture flows from the top. As a leader, your actions and decisions set the tone for the entire organisation. Model the behaviours and values you want to see in your team.

Dare to Reimagine Hiring

Hiring for culture fit isn't about finding people who merely blend in; it's about discovering those who will amplify and evolve your culture. By daring to reimagine every step of the hiring process, from job descriptions to onboarding, you can build a team that not only aligns with your mission but propels it forward. Culture fit is the difference between employees who clock in and out and those who champion your vision with passion and purpose. When you invest in hiring for culture, you're not just building a team; you're creating a legacy.

Rewrite One Job Description Today

Pick the next open role (or one you've recently filled). Now, rewrite the job description using these principles:

- Speak in your company's tone of voice.

- Share your "why" and your team culture.

- Be honest. Name one area the company is still improving. End with this sentence: "We don't expect perfection, but rather we're looking for someone who aligns with our values and wants to grow with us." Maybe above all else, this sentence, with its hint of vulnerability, can attract exactly the kind of candidate you need.

These actions don't require fancy HR systems or corporate consultants. They require intention. Hiring for culture fit isn't just a process; rather, it's a practice. One that can transform your business from a collection of employees into a united force with shared energy and purpose.

Chapter 4

Strategies for Employee Engagement

RECOGNISING AND CELEBRATING ACHIEVEMENTS

Let's pause and reflect for a moment. When was the last time you celebrated a win with your team? Recognition isn't just a pat on the back; it's a powerful driver of motivation and engagement. Think of it like fuel for the fire. Acknowledging achievements keeps the flames of enthusiasm and commitment burning bright. As Dale Carnegie, paraphrasing William James, wisely observed, "The deepest craving of human nature is the need to be appreciated". Recognition is more than an acknowledgement; it reinforces value and contribution.

> Research shows that employees who feel recognised are 63% more likely to stay at their current job (*Gallup, 2017*).

Consider the example of Salesforce, where a formal peer-to-peer recognition programme called Gong allows employees to celebrate each other's achievements in a highly visible and meaningful way. This simple system has contributed to Salesforce's reputation as one of the best places to work globally (Salesforce, 2020). Maybe you don't want to go quite that far, but it doesn't have to be a formal system. Many employees can be reluctant to speak their minds in those rigidly defined environments. When I opened my first factory in 1980, I called it "Management by Walking About." However, all credit goes to Tom Peters and Robert Waterman, who popularised the phrase "Management by Walking Around" (MBWA) in their 1982 book *In Search of*

Excellence (Peters and Waterman, 1982). The concept was based on their observation that successful leaders spent time interacting with employees and walking around the organisation. And boy, were they right!

Begin by focusing on the milestones that truly matter. These might be big victories, like hitting a major target, or quieter moments, like a team member mastering a new skill. The size of the achievement doesn't matter; what matters is showing that you notice and appreciate their efforts. Sometimes, a simple thank you can mean more than you realise. You can double the effectiveness of that thank you by making sure the recipient knows they have been truly noticed. Let me give you an example: On Tuesday morning, you thank Robert, a machine operator, for working late to finish a job the previous evening. He is pleased to receive your thanks. Then, on Friday, his line manager tells him that the CEO had been saying what a great job Robert had done and what a difference his efforts had made. Now, let me ask you a question: Is Robert likely to be putting in his notice soon? I don't think so.

The right structure can help make recognition a consistent part of your culture. Consider setting aside time during team meetings to highlight accomplishments or creating a formal programme to reward excellence. Reinforce that by taking every opportunity to have informal chats. These gestures reinforce the idea that every contribution matters and build a sense of camaraderie. But a word of warning: taken too far, these kinds of meetings, particularly the more formal ones, can be seen as patronising or viewed cynically by team members who question your motives.

Recognition is most impactful when it's personal. Tailor your approach to what resonates with your team. Some might prefer public accolades, while others might value a one-on-one conversation or a handwritten note. By taking the time to acknowledge achievements in ways that feel meaningful, you demonstrate to your team that you recognise and value them.

There is one more thing to consider. Recognition is a shared responsibility; it shouldn't just flow from the top down, but in all directions—and I mean ALL directions.. We should never underestimate the beneficial impact of peer-to-peer recognition. It has the power to transform team dynamics. The dog-eat-dog world of trying to get ahead at the expense of one's workmates can become a thing of the past.

Now, let's look at recognition that defies gravity and flows upwards. So you're the boss, eh? Looking down on everyone from your ivory tower? Starting today, take the metaphorical bars from your windows. As soon as you start showing that you really care, you'll be amazed at the recognition and loyalty that comes your way. Oh, and a word of warning: when it does, you'd better brace yourself for just how good it makes you feel.

LOOK FOR THE WHY BEHIND THE WOW.

Here's another thought. Go beyond the gold star sticker method. Don't just say, "Wow, what a great job!" Look for the why behind the wow. Why did something make you say "Wow"? What effect or impact did that action have on you, your organisation, or even the world at large?

FAILURES

What about failures? True recognition embraces the courage to try. I know this is hard, but see every failure as a stepping stone, and make sure that the person who feels responsible for the failure knows that too. Let them know that we only learn and grow through failure, and when you say it, MEAN IT. When members of my staff came to me telling me that they had failed or messed up, my comment was usually something like, "If that's the worst mistake you make this month, I can live with that." I admit that those words might sometimes have been delivered through gritted teeth, but generally, as far as I was concerned, it was a win. At least it meant they were trying.

BEYOND THE COMPANY'S WALLS

Here's another thought for you. Amplify recognition beyond the company's walls. If they're willing, share employees' achievements on your website or social media channels. Nominate them for industry awards; showcase their excellence and how proud you are of them. You might fear that doing such things will make them a target for being headhunted by rivals, and you'd probably be right. However, chances are that they will become ambassadors for your business. They will know to their core that they are in the right place.

EMPOWERING THROUGH AUTONOMY

Let me ask you: What happens when you give your team the space to take ownership of their work? Autonomy isn't about stepping back and letting go; it's about empowering your employees to take the lead and make decisions. It's about showing them you trust their judgment and believe in their abilities.

Peter Drucker once said, "The most serious mistakes are not being made as a result of wrong answers. The true danger is in asking the wrong questions" (Drucker, n.d.). This insight reminds us that autonomy enables innovation and growth by encouraging employees to ask and answer meaningful questions. Ownership grows when you foster an environment of trust and support. Be there as a guide, not a micromanager. Check in regularly to provide encouragement and remove obstacles, but let them own their successes, and even their mistakes. Growth happens when people feel safe to try, fail, and try again.

As we sit here, imagine what your business could achieve with a team that's motivated not just by your direction but by their own sense of purpose. Autonomy and ownership don't just engage employees; they transform them into leaders in their own right.

PROVIDING OPPORTUNITIES FOR GROWTH

Think back to a time when you learned something new that changed how you approached your work. That feeling of growth and possibility is what we want to give your team. Opportunities for growth aren't just a perk; they're a cornerstone of engagement. When people see a path for development, they're more invested in their work and your business.

Benjamin Franklin said: "Without continual growth and progress, such words as improvement, achievement, and success have no meaning" (Franklin, n.d.). Growth opportunities align personal aspirations with organisational goals.

According to LinkedIn's *Workplace Learning Report* (2021), 94% of employees said they would stay longer at a company that invested in their learning and development (*LinkedIn, 2021*).

Start by having conversations with your team about their aspirations. What skills do they want to build? Where do they see themselves in a year, five years, or ten? These discussions aren't just about identifying training opportunities; they're about showing your team that you care about their futures. And, as I said earlier and will probably say again, when I say "care", I mean really care. Pretending to care is not only patronising, it can also be destructive.

Mentorship is another powerful tool for growth. Pairing experienced team members with those seeking to learn fosters a culture of knowledge sharing and collaboration. Both mentors and mentees gain something valuable, whether it's refining their skills or gaining fresh perspectives.

Don't forget to celebrate the journey. When a team member completes a course, masters a new system, or takes on a challenging project, take the time to acknowledge their effort and progress. These moments build confidence and reinforce the value of continuous improvement.

Providing growth opportunities isn't just about advancing skills; it's about creating a workplace where people feel they're growing alongside the business. When your team grows, so does your business's potential.

A QUICK STORY

Imagine that you're sitting in a bar. (Some will find that easier than others, but who am I to judge?) You've called in to meet some friends for a drink after work. While you are waiting for them to arrive, you strike up a conversation with someone who, it seems, drives for a trucking company. He proceeds to bemoan the fact that he hates his job, blaming his bad bosses and the shoddy service they provide. The following week, you are once again waiting for your friends to arrive, and once again, you find yourself in conversation with someone who drives for a different trucking company. He has nothing but praise for them. He loves his job and is clearly proud to work for them. Neither driver had a clue that you were looking to appoint a new haulage contractor. Both companies had tendered for your contract. Having spoken to two members of their staff, which company are you more likely to do business with? The second driver had become an ambassador for the business he works for. He and people like him are the ultimate sales force.

POINTS TO PONDER

Introduce "Spotlight Moments" in Team Meetings

Whether it's in scheduled team meetings or informal gatherings, dedicate five minutes to "Spotlight Moments" to give shoutouts to individual achievements, big or small. But here's the twist: the person giving the praise must explain why it mattered. Not just "Great job", but "It saved the client relationship", "It lifted the mood", "It showed courage." This deepens the impact because it's recognition with resonance.

Create a Peer-to-Peer Recognition Wall

Encourage your team to post brief, sincere notes to each other. It could be an app, a Slack channel, or, my personal favourite, a pinboard for all to see. Keep it informal and optional. Don't force it, but rather nurture it. When it starts to build momentum organically, you've just rewired your culture for mutual respect.

Start "MBWA" Lite

Set aside a few minutes every day if you can. Just walk around or do quick video check-ins to check in (not to check up).

I am not suggesting that you formalise those check-ins by asking the questions below. Direct questions can elicit answers that the respondent thinks you want to hear. It's much better to have the questions in mind when engaging team members in conversation. Show them that you care about what they have to say.

- What's going well for you this week?

- Anything making your job harder than it needs to be?

- Who do you think deserves a thank-you?

Make a point of remembering what you hear; it's gold dust for recognition and process improvement.

Celebrate Failures That Had Courage

Start a "Well-Tried Award". This light-hearted attention is a sincere way to recognise a team member who took a risk, tried something new, or put their hand up to lead. Let the team know: "Trying matters here, even if it doesn't go perfectly." This builds safety, resilience, and a real spirit of learning.

There is a strong, however, here. On occasions, a failure might give rise to laughter. If that is kindly laughter, then that is probably okay, but if it descends into derision, that is certainly NOT okay. Let's say the person being laughed at is called Bob. Nip such things in the bud by pointing out, directly to those laughing, "At least Bob tried, and that is what I admire and want to see in all of you." Be seen to be standing up for Bob and for anyone else who demonstrates courage to try something new.

Go Public With Praise

If it's appropriate (and with their permission), share a story of one team member's achievement on your website, internal newsletter, or even your LinkedIn. Bonus points if you tag or credit them directly. The pride it builds isn't just theirs; the whole team feels it. You don't need PR spin. Just tell it like you'd tell a friend at a party.

Ownership Challenges

Pick one upcoming project or decision. Hand over part of it to a team member with this message: "I trust your judgment. Own this. Make the call. I've got your back." Stay involved just enough to be supportive, but let them lead. Watch how this changes how they walk into work the next day.

Initiate "Growth Conversations"

Turn performance reviews into growth conversations. Ask:

- What would you love to learn?

- What project would challenge you in a good way?

- Where do you see yourself growing next?

Show them you're not just focused on what they do for you, but what you can do for their future.

Pilot a Mini Mentorship Scheme

Pair up junior and senior team members for 2–3 months. Keep it informal: one coffee catch-up or Zoom every week or so. Be sure to let them know that the conversation is a two-way street. There will be things that the senior team member can learn, too. Offer guiding questions if needed, like "What do you wish you'd known in your first year here?" Mentorship quietly builds trust, learning, and continuity of culture.

Measure Engagement Ambassadorship

Ask yourself this bold question each month: "If my team members met a stranger in a bar, how would they describe working here?"

Then, ask one or two team members the exact same question. Their answers will tell you where your culture truly stands and where you need to dig deeper.

Chapter 5

Enhancing Team Communication

ESTABLISHING OPEN COMMUNICATION CHANNELS

Open communication isn't just a goal; it's the foundation of any thriving workplace. When communication flows freely, trust grows, and collaboration becomes second nature. Let's talk about how to create those open channels, where everyone feels heard and understood.

> Just so you know, I'm not making this up - research has shown that organisations with highly effective communication practices are 50% more likely to have lower employee turnover rates (*McKinsey, 2017*).

Start by modelling the behaviour you want to see. In other words, be the change you want to see. Are you approachable? Do your team members feel comfortable coming to you with ideas, questions, or concerns? Peter Drucker's insight captures the importance of attentiveness in communication: "The most important thing in communication is to hear what isn't being said." You need to cultivate the skill of perceiving unspoken concerns, which often carry significant weight. Listen with your eyes as well as your ears.

Make time for regular one-on-one check-ins and team meetings where dialogue is actively encouraged. These spaces aren't just for updates; they're opportunities to connect, align, and grow together. Make use of tools that enhance communication, whether it's a messaging platform like Slack for quick questions or a shared workspace for collaborative projects. Prioritise openness and transparency, and the tools will amplify those values.

ENCOURAGING FEEDBACK AND DIALOGUE

Let's think about feedback for a moment. How do you feel when someone genuinely listens to you? It builds connection, doesn't it? Now, imagine creating that same sense of connection within your team. Feedback isn't just about evaluation, it's about dialogue. It's about making your team feel seen, heard, and valued. Remember, it's not just what we say, it's about how we act and what we do.

Ken Blanchard summed it up nicely: "Feedback is the breakfast of champions." Regular, constructive feedback fuels improvement and growth. Start by framing feedback as a two-way street. Let your team know that their opinions are valued. Encourage them to share their ideas, concerns, and suggestions regularly. Whether it's during team meetings, in casual conversations, or through structured feedback sessions, create spaces where dialogue feels natural and safe.

When you give feedback, focus on being constructive and supportive. Highlight both strengths and areas for growth, and always tie your feedback to the bigger picture.

> Research from the Corporate Leadership Council shows that employees who receive regular, constructive feedback are 23% more likely to perform at higher levels (*CLC, 2020*).

Act on the feedback you receive. Even small changes based on team suggestions can have a huge impact. When your team sees that their input leads to tangible results, trust grows, and engagement deepens.

Feedback and dialogue aren't just tools; they're the bridges that connect you with your team. Fostering these connections will do much to help create a workplace where collaboration and trust thrive.

A quick example: In the 1970s (yes, I am that old), I had just completed an apprenticeship at a large steel plant. A plant safety committee was set up to look at issues from the employees' perspective. I was sent to represent the lower echelons of the head office. A steel plant is a highly dangerous environment. One particular hazard revolved around the heavy lorries that manoeuvred steel around the plant. There had been several close calls as they reversed. I suggested that it would be relatively simple to link the vehicle's reversing light to an alarm. When the driver selected reverse and the reversing light was turned on, the same supply could trigger a reversing alarm, warning pedestrians that the vehicle was in reverse. I was 19 years old. The senior management scoffed at my suggestion, branding it a "stupid idea." I never bothered to make any more suggestions. All these years later, such alarms have become standard practice. Maybe I missed my first entrepreneurial opportunity at that point.

THE SILO ISSUE

As organisations grow, so too does the size, number, and often complexity of the different departments within them. While senior management might perceive the organisation pulling in the same direction as they view it from the top floor, seen from below, this can be anything but the case.

Departments can become isolated and seek to serve only their own interests, which can detract from the business as a whole. In the extreme, departments might "go to war" with each other. Salvos of distrust and venom are fired from silo to silo. Once this kind of thing has taken root, it can be difficult, if not impossible, to rectify without major surgery. The answer is, of course, not to let it take root in the first place. This is where communication can truly shine, breaking down silos with effective cross-team communication. How do we do that? I hear you ask. It's all about getting rid of the "us and them" mindset.

Here are a few suggestions:

- Establish a cross-team contact initiative – involve all of the teams (would-be silos) from the start. Randomly pair employees from different departments to work on a problem or issue that might typically have nothing to do with them. The aim is to foster cross-border friendships and ultimately demonstrate how departments contribute to the "big picture."

- Reward initiatives that might not directly help, indeed might detract from, an individual department, but benefit the business as a whole.

- Create social gatherings where there is news to share. Yes, accountants can be seen to socialise with the sales team, I promise!

CONSTRUCTIVE CONFLICT

A word on constructive conflict, whatever that means.

Healthy conflict is good; some would argue essential for innovation. Create a culture where disagreements are seen as opportunities for growth, rather than threats. Celebrate instances where an argument or disagreement results in a better outcome than would have been achieved by staying silent. Quiet acceptance allows second-rate practice to creep in and become the norm.

UTILISING TECHNOLOGY FOR SEAMLESS COMMUNICATION

Technology is a game-changer when it comes to communication, but it's not the whole story. It's the way you use technology that makes the difference. Think of it as the instrument, with you and your team creating the music.

"Technology is best when it brings people together," a sentiment that highlights its role as a connector rather than a mere tool. Platforms like Microsoft Teams and Zoom have revolutionised how remote teams collaborate, enabling real-time communication and effective virtual meetings.

A study by Frost & Sullivan found that businesses adopting unified communication tools see a 25% increase in productivity (*Frost & Sullivan, 2021*).

Set guidelines for using these tools to ensure clarity and reduce overwhelm. For example, decide which platform is best for quick updates and which is better for in-depth discussions. Clear expectations make communication more efficient and reduce misunderstandings.

Technology can also be a powerful tool for recognition and feedback. Utilise platforms that enable peer-to-peer recognition or offer spaces for anonymous suggestions. These features make it easier for your team to stay engaged and connected.

However, remember that no tool can replace the value of a heartfelt conversation or a face-to-face check-in. Technology is there to support you, not to replace you. By using it thoughtfully, you create a seamless flow of communication that keeps your team aligned and motivated.

As we sit here, let's imagine your business as a finely tuned orchestra, each part working in harmony because communication is clear and strong. Technology can be the conductor's baton, but that baton is in your hands.

POINTS TO PONDER

Turn Communication into Connection

Ask yourself honestly: "Am I approachable?" Do a self-audit. When did you last:

- Invite an idea from someone who is usually quiet?

- Thank someone for honest criticism?

- Acknowledge that you don't have all the answers?

These actions speak louder than any comms plan. Start small, but start.

Listen With Intent

Create space for one-to-one meetings and informal chats that focus not just on tasks, but on how your team members are feeling.

Have these questions in mind. You may ask them directly, but that runs the risk of being given the answers you want to hear. It's sometimes better to tease out the answers in a relaxed conversation.

- What's working well for you right now?

- Is anything slowing you down or frustrating you?

- Is there something you wish you could say but haven't?

Listen not just with your ears, but with your eyes and heart. Don't interrupt. Don't fix. Just hear them.

Start a "Feedback is Fuel" Habit

In every meeting this month, ask one question that invites feedback. Example questions might include:

- What should we stop doing?

- What could we do better together?

Be open to what you hear, even if it stings. *Especially* if it stings. That's where growth lives.

Use the "Why Behind the Wow" Rule

When you give praise, go deeper.

Instead of saying *"Great job on the report!"* Explain what benefits it brought.

The considerable weight this adds to any praise or applause cannot be overstated.

Break Down Silos With Cross-Team Challenges

Choose a real issue (it doesn't have to be mission-critical. Form pairs or trios from different departments and task them with exploring solutions together. Give a deadline, offer a little support, then stand back to see how cross-pollination can build empathy, awareness, and even unearth unexpected brilliance.

Introduce a "Constructive Conflict Showcase"

Ask team members to share examples (anonymised if needed) where disagreement led to a better solution. Celebrate the conflict that created clarity. Over time, you'll normalise speaking up as an act of courage, not insubordination.

Set Up "Comms Tool Clarity" Guidelines

Don't let digital tools become digital noise.

As a team, decide:

- Which tools are for urgent vs. non-urgent communications.

- What deserves a meeting vs. a message.

- What should always be said face-to-face or via video.

Stick to it. These small agreements create big improvements in how people feel and work.

Agree with the team on a tool/platform for social chat. It's going to happen anyway if you are going to create the closely knit team you seek. If social chat clutters the other channels, it will rob them of their efficiency and possibly cause resentment when you curtail it.

Don't be a hypocrite and use the wrong channel just because it's convenient. How can you expect others to follow rules if you don't?

Create a "Silent Alarm" Culture

Remember Drucker's wisdom: "The most important thing in communication is to hear what isn't being said."

Encourage your managers to watch for withdrawal, silence, or sudden disengagement. These are often signs that someone is struggling to speak up.

Make "I noticed you've been quiet. How are you?" a regular question, and don't accept the first answer if it's clearly not true.

Share Tech Wins, Not Just Features

If your team is using platforms like Slack, MS Teams, or Zoom, showcase real stories of how those tools helped someone collaborate, solve a problem, or feel connected. Stories inspire far better adoption than training manuals ever could.

Tell the "Reversing Alarm" Story

Share the reversing alarm story I recounted earlier in this chapter (or a similar one) when onboarding a new person. Let them know:

- Their voice matters.

- Even unpolished ideas can shape the future.

- Let that be part of the DNA of your communication culture from day one.

These action points aren't shiny corporate communication strategies. They're grounded, human, and they work. Because in the end, communication isn't about words. It's about connection, courage, and consistency.

Chapter 6

Trust Building Within Teams

THE ROLE OF TRUST IN TEAM SUCCESS

Let's add a couple more logs to the fire and continue. Picture this: your team operating like a well-oiled machine, everyone confident in their role and the support of their colleagues. Trust is the foundation that makes this possible. Without it, even the most talented team can struggle. Let's take a moment to explore how trust transforms a group of individuals into a cohesive, high-performing unit.

Stephen Covey famously said, "Trust is the glue of life. It's the most essential ingredient in effective communication. It's the foundational principle that holds all relationships." Trust is central to team dynamics, influencing everything from communication to collaboration.

> A study by PwC found that employees in high-trust organisations are 74% less stressed and 50% more productive compared to those in low-trust environments. This isn't just a feel-good statistic; it's a business imperative (*PwC, 2018*).

Take Netflix, for example. The company's "Freedom and Responsibility" policy places immense trust in employees, offering unlimited vacation time and encouraging autonomy. This trust translates into high performance and innovation, cementing Netflix's position as an industry leader. Perhaps the thought of going that far makes you shudder, but it's an interesting concept, don't you think?

Trust begins with you. As the leader, your actions set the tone for the entire organization. Are you consistent in your words and actions? Do you follow through on commitments? When your team sees you acting with integrity and reliability, they feel safe to do the same. Trust starts with transparency, sharing not just the wins but also the challenges. When you're honest about where the business stands and where it's headed, your team feels included and valued.

That being said, I must add a word of caution. There can be such a thing as over-sharing. An everyday problem for you can seem like the end of the world to someone who is less able to cope with the stress. You may be confident that it can be dealt with, but unless you can properly reassure them, you will find them scrolling through job sites. If they feel insecure and leave, they damage the business, and their behaviour becomes a self-fulfilling prophecy.

Staff may not be looking to jump ship, but those who are not easily able to cope with what they have learned will likely be stressed and may be in fear of losing their job. And when stress and fear walk through the door, the ability to make sensible decisions and stay creative jumps out of the window, along with any enjoyment they ever had in the job. As the absentee level goes up, it passes productivity levels that are on their way down.

Share, but don't overshare if it will make them feel insecure. However, there may be times when you have no alternative but to make full disclosure, those occasions when it has to be all hands to the pumps if you are to survive. They may be like rats deserting a sinking ship, but if they stay and you survive, what a team you'll have!

STRATEGIES FOR BUILDING TRUST

Let's break it down. How do you actually build trust? It's a question worth asking because trust is at the core of everything your business achieves.

Ernest Hemingway offers a stunningly simple insight: "The best way to find out if you can trust somebody is to trust them." Extending trust proactively creates a foundation for reciprocation within a team. Start with accountability. Hold yourself and your team to the same standards. When everyone knows that they can rely on one another, trust naturally grows. Be clear about expectations and celebrate those who meet or exceed them. At the same time, be fair and constructive when someone falls short. Consistency builds credibility.

It's no surprise that communication is key. Keep the lines of dialogue open. Regular one-on-one check-ins and team meetings provide opportunities to address concerns, share updates, and reinforce shared goals. When your team knows that they can come to you with anything, trust deepens.

Show appreciation. Acknowledging the efforts of your team, whether through a public shout-out or a personal thank-you, reinforces the idea that their contributions matter. Trust thrives in an environment where people feel valued and respected. I will say that again, 'cos it's important. Trust thrives in an environment where people feel valued and respected.

Finally, lead with empathy. Take the time to understand the perspectives and challenges of your team members. When people feel seen and supported, they're more likely to extend that trust to you and their peers. Empathy is a powerful, if not the ultimate, tool for fostering connections and creating a resilient team.

OVERCOMING TRUST BARRIERS

What if trust has been broken? It happens. The good news is that trust, while fragile, is also rebuildable. The key is to address issues head-on with honesty and a commitment to repair.

Start by acknowledging the problem. If trust has been eroded, don't ignore it. Have open conversations about what went wrong and what can be done to fix it. Your willingness to address the issue sets the tone for rebuilding.

C.S. Lewis captured the essence of rebuilding trust when he said, "'Integrity is doing the right thing, even when no one is watching." Consistently acting with integrity rebuilds confidence in leadership and sets an example for the entire team.

Be patient. Trust takes time to recover. Focus on consistent, trustworthy behaviour and provide opportunities for your team to see you following through on your commitments. Small actions, repeated over time, can rebuild even the most damaged relationships.

As I write this section, just yesterday, I was asked to sit in on a meeting that was likely to be contentious. Two managers had suddenly become at loggerheads. Both were convinced of their case; they believed they were right, and the other was wrong. Trust had been eroded, but a lack of communication meant the situation had gone unnoticed. Soon after the meeting began, it became clear that there was little hope of immediate reconciliation. Gradually, the argument subsided, but the distrust and, by then, dislike, remained. We had to be pragmatic. It was clear that there was no magic pill that could bring them together. We explored and eventually found areas where they could work independently of each other with only the rarest of contact. In taking what might be called a "small steps" option, we temporarily lowered our acceptable outcome parameters in the hope that their relationship would heal over time. However, there was a strong caveat to the proposal. If it was failing, and the fractious situation allowed to spill over to affect the organisation as a whole, then more drastic action would be needed.

My point is this – it's all very well for writers like me to offer panaceas and solutions to head off problems before they occur. That might be fine on paper, but business isn't played on paper; it's played on a pitch. Sometimes, uncomfortable as it may be, we have to keep digging until we find a solution. Accept the fact that it might not be complete, but a work in progress.

Reinforce positivity. Highlight the progress you're making as a team and celebrate milestones together. These shared moments remind everyone of the potential and strength that can be achieved when working together.

As we sit here, let's imagine your business thriving in a culture of trust. It's not just about fixing what's broken, it's about building something even stronger than before. Trust is the glue that binds a team together, and with intention, you can make it unshakable.

POINTS TO PONDER

Create a Feedback Loop

Create a feedback loop where team leaders can ask how recent events, their recent decisions, or actions have fostered or perhaps eroded trust. Make a point of doing this exercise when things are going well – it can have a magnifying effect on dissatisfaction if these conversations are started at the wrong time.

Play the Empathy Game.

Encourage and participate in the game of seeing recent events through another's eyes. For example, ask a recent junior employee to help you understand their perspective on a recent slump in production. Has it affected his wages? Has it had an effect at home? If so, in what way? Or ask the sales manager to spend time with the finance manager so that he can come to understand the ripple effect of a good or bad deal he has struck. Of course, it's a two-way street here; the finance manager might grow to understand the stresses of selling.

The only way, as I see it, that the empathy game might fall down is if you ask a newly started junior employee to see things through the CEO's eyes. Chances are, they won't understand the concepts that the CEO deals with every day. If they do at that early stage in their career, then the CEO might just have found their successor.

Recognize and Applaud Integrity

Make a point of recognizing and applauding integrity – when someone has *done the right thing,* even if it was to the detriment of the business. Go deeper than simple applause and reinforce why it's being applauded by explaining the benefit that the demonstration of integrity has brought. Get others involved in that conversation. Encourage them to show how it helps them carry out their job, perhaps how it makes them proud to be part of the team.

Chapter 7

Leadership Development for Team Success

IDENTIFYING LEADERSHIP QUALITIES

In looking for people to hire, you look for three qualities: integrity, intelligence, and energy. If they don't have the first, the other two will kill you.

— Warren Buffett

Let's sit back for a moment and reflect on what makes a great leader. It's not just about authority or decision-making. It's about inspiring others to believe in the vision and in their own abilities to contribute to it. True leadership transforms teams, and the best part? Leadership isn't reserved for a select few. It's a skill anyone can develop with intention and effort.

EMOTIONAL INTELLIGENCE AS A CORNERSTONE OF LEADERSHIP

Leaders with high emotional intelligence understand their own emotions and the emotions of others. They create environments where people feel seen, heard, and supported. Maya Angelou captured this sentiment beautifully: "I've learned that people will forget what you said, people will forget what you did, but people will never forget how you made them feel." By showing empathy and emotional awareness, leaders leave lasting impacts on their teams.

Take the example of Satya Nadella, CEO of Microsoft, who transformed the company's culture by focusing on adaptability and a growth mindset. His leadership reinvigorated innovation and collaboration across the organisation (*Microsoft, 2020*).

Adaptability is another essential quality. The ability to pivot, embrace change, and lead through uncertainty inspires confidence. An insight, widely attributed to Charles Darwin, speaks to this perfectly: "It is not the strongest of the species that survive, nor the most intelligent, but the one most responsive to change." *(Megginson, 1963)* When a leader is flexible, the team feels secure, knowing they can weather any storm together.

Integrity ties everything together. A leader who acts with honesty and consistency builds unshakable trust. When your team knows you'll always act in their best interest and align with the business's values, they're more likely to follow your lead. Warren Buffett once said, "In looking for people to hire, you look for three qualities: integrity, intelligence, and energy. If they don't have the first, the other two will kill you" (*Buffett, 1994*).

Lastly, vision is what sets leaders apart. Leaders don't just see where the business is. They see where it can go. Helen Keller's words are a powerful reminder of this: "The only thing worse than being blind is having sight but no vision." A visionary leader inspires their team to reach shared goals, guiding them toward a compelling future. What about you? How can you refine and share your vision to inspire those around you? The most important word here is "inspire". Think about the great leaders in history; what made them great?

MENTORSHIP AND COACHING FOR GROWTH

Next time you are speaking with a member of your team, set your boss's hat to one side and think of yourself as their mentor. You're not just guiding their tasks, you're investing in their growth. Mentorship and coaching are powerful tools for unlocking potential and building strong, resilient teams.

Mentorship fosters a space for knowledge sharing and connection. Pair experienced team members with those looking to grow and watch how both parties flourish.

> For instance, AT&T's mentorship program is designed to prepare employees for future leadership roles, resulting in higher engagement and retention rates (*AT&T, 2018*).

The mentor sharpens their leadership skills, while the mentee gains insights and confidence. It's a win-win that strengthens your entire team.

Coaching, on the other hand, is a more structured approach. It's about setting goals, identifying obstacles, and working together to overcome them. As a coach, your role is to listen deeply, ask thoughtful questions, and provide encouragement.

> Research from the International Coaching Federation indicates that companies implementing coaching practices experience a 70% improvement in individual performance (*ICF, 2019*).

Coaching doesn't just improve performance, but rather it builds trust and loyalty.

When mentorship and coaching become part of your culture, your team becomes more engaged, motivated, and willing to step into leadership roles themselves. That's how you create a ripple effect of development throughout your business.

EMPOWERING LEADERS WITHIN TEAMS

Now, let's talk about empowerment. Imagine a team where leadership isn't confined to titles but is shared across all levels. Empowering leaders within your team is about giving people the tools, confidence, and autonomy to step up when it matters most.

Start by identifying potential leaders. These aren't always the loudest voices in the room, but rather they're the ones who listen, who step in to help without being asked, and who inspire others by their example. When you spot these qualities, nurture them. Provide these individuals with opportunities to lead projects, make decisions, and take ownership of their outcomes. You may have to do it quietly, coax them out of their reticence and embarrassment of being singled out by the boss.

Empowerment thrives on trust. Show your team that you believe in their abilities by giving them the freedom to act. Be there to guide them, but resist the urge to micromanage. When people feel trusted, they rise to the occasion. One of my most productive phrases when it came to individual team member development was: "I have more faith in you than you have in yourself." I do not claim that this sentence has an immediate effect, but repeated over time, I have seen individuals blossom into something they never believed possible.

Leadership development is also about providing resources. Offer training, mentorship, and feedback that help your team grow to their potential. Celebrate their successes, and when they stumble, be the safety net that helps them bounce back stronger.

As we sit here, think about what your business could achieve with a team full of empowered leaders. When leadership is shared, the possibilities are endless. Your role isn't to lead alone; it's to create an environment where everyone has the chance to lead.

POINTS TO PONDER

Adaptability

Think about the Charles Darwin quotation mentioned earlier. When change is being sought or forced upon us, hold sessions (whether they are one-on-one or group sessions, it doesn't matter) to reinforce how important adaptability is not only for evolution and growth, but also for survival.

The Meaning of Integrity

Make a point of getting to know what integrity means to your team leaders. Do they understand how important it is as a compass of leadership? Encourage them to carry out the same exercise with individuals in their teams.

Welcome Every Idea

Encourage visionary thinking. Welcome every idea. What seems radical or stupid today could become the norm tomorrow.

Mentoring Both Ways

Explore the idea of reverse mentoring. Encourage senior leaders, including yourself, to sit in with junior employees. You may well not agree with everything they say, but the insights you'll come away with might just be the gem you've been looking for.

Play the Delegation Game

Delegate, delegate, delegate. The only way to know we can trust someone to carry out tasks is actually to take a risk on them. Play the game: "What can I delegate for a day?" See how it goes. If it's a failure, then you've lost little, but if it's a success, you've gained precious time to concentrate on other things. Ask your team leaders to follow your example throughout the organisation. But of course, we can't, or at least shouldn't, delegate a task and leave people to flounder. They have to know that you are there to help them should they be struggling. Just as importantly, know that you won't judge them as a failure. The challenge with delegation isn't just one of trust; it's one of time! "It's quicker just to do it myself," we say, and of course, chances are that's right. But it's not quicker to do it yourself when you're doing it the next dozen times and on into the future, when someone else would by then be doing it for you.

Vulnerability Pays Dividends

Model vulnerability as a strength. It's the ultimate bridge builder towards trust and connection. Encourage everyone to share their struggles, but once again, a word of warning: don't let it become a licence to moan! "Woe is me" is not what everyone wants to hear. Celebrate a culture where it's okay to be radical, even if the outcome is less than perfect, and where challenges and roadblocks are seen as stepping stones to the future.

Well-Being

Make a point of prioritising well-being as a leadership imperative. Monitor the emotional states of your team both formally and informally. Set clear limits on work hours and let team members know the reason why these limits are there. All this helps maintain that oft-used phrase, "A healthy work-life balance." That's not just a throwaway statement; it's key to maintaining morale and can pay for itself many times over in improved productivity and a reduction in absenteeism. Let's not forget staff churn. We all know how expensive that can be.

Possibilities Not Limitations

I know I've said this before, but I'll say it again. With every conversation you have, focus on possibilities rather than limitations. Think "Here's what we can do" as opposed to, 'Here's what we can't do."

The Wonders of Recognition

Once again, I'm repeating myself. Recognise achievements at every opportunity. You will be amazed at how this reinforces a sense of purpose, possibility, and loyalty. Don't just whisper those recognitions, shout them from the highest tree tops. Spread the message far and wide within your organisation.

Resilience—A Pillar of Success

Prioritise resilience. Don't just talk the talk, walk the walk. The legacy you create will be one of strength, adaptability, and enduring impact.

Chapter 8

Measuring Engagement and Motivation

IDENTIFYING KEY PERFORMANCE INDICATORS

Peter Drucker, famously known as the father of management, is widely attributed to having said, "What gets measured gets managed." (Although, in the interests of academic accuracy, this should be attributed to others) *(Kaplan and Norton, 1992)*. How do you measure progress? What tells you whether the team is thriving or struggling? This is where key performance indicators (KPIs) come into play. Selecting the right KPIs ensures that your efforts to enhance engagement are focused and effective. Start by identifying ones that align with your vision and values. KPIs aren't just metrics; they can be the compass guiding your decisions and showing you how engaged and motivated your team truly is. Think beyond productivity. Consider metrics like employee retention rates and participation in team activities.

> A Gallup poll in 2017 recorded 22% higher profitability and 21% higher productivity as a result of increased team activities. Who in their right mind wouldn't want to see those kinds of improvements (*Gallup, 2017*)?

Involve your team in setting these KPIs. Ask them what matters most and what success looks like from their point of view.

> By shifting away from annual performance reviews to a continuous feedback system, Adobe saw a 30% reduction in voluntary turnover (*Adobe, 2018*).

When employees have a hand in defining the benchmarks, they're more likely to feel invested in achieving them. We're not just talking about numbers here; there should be a qualitative element. KPIs are stories about your team's engagement and motivation.

CONDUCTING EMPLOYEE SURVEYS

Sometimes, the best way to understand your team is to simply ask questions. Employee surveys are like holding a mirror up to your organisation. They reflect the thoughts, feelings, and needs of the people who drive your business forward. Alan Mulally, former CEO of Ford, once said, "The customer is the most important part of the assembly line." Adapted internally, this wisdom reminds us that our employees are at the heart of our success. Surveys should focus on areas that matter most: job satisfaction, communication, leadership, and opportunities for growth. Use a mix of open-ended questions and rating scales. For example, some consultants or experts would suggest asking, "On a scale of 1 to 10, how connected do you feel to the organisation's mission?" Then have you follow that with an open-ended question: "What could strengthen that connection?"

> According to a study by the Society for Human Resource Management (SHRM), organisations that conduct regular employee surveys experience a 40% improvement in engagement (*SHRM, 2020*).

A word of caution, though. If your team is relatively small (or even if it isn't), this kind of approach can backfire. It presupposes an understanding of the organisation's mission. We have to first engage with people to ensure they have that understanding. Only then can we assess the degree to which they "buy in" to it. As for assessing on a scale of 1–10, be careful that it doesn't come across as a cold statistics-gathering exercise. In smaller organisations or teams, when staff are there working alongside you every day, you have ample opportunities to naturally glean the kind of information a survey of a larger team might provide. The 1–10 exercise can seem like you are building your ivory tower, driving a wedge between you and them. We want to get to the "why" and "why not" of any connection gap. Listen with both ears to how it can be closed. This isn't about numbers and statistics, it's about people.

Whether you choose the formal survey approach or the less formal conversational approach, once you gather responses, it's time to act. Share the results with your team, highlighting both the positives and the areas that need improvement. Be transparent about what you're addressing and how. Even small changes based on feedback can have a significant impact on morale and trust.

> Google implemented a team feedback mechanism called "Project Aristotle," which revealed that psychological safety was the most important factor in team success. (*Bock, 2015*).

Studies have shown that peer-to-peer support is critical to maintaining a healthy team. It isn't just about you showing that you care about them, it's about creating a family where they care about each other, and most importantly of all, every one of them knows that to be true. In what I consider to be one of the best management books ever written, "The Happiness Advantage", author Sean Achor wrote, "When we encounter an unexpected challenge or threat, the only way to save ourselves is to hold on tight to the people around us and not let go." And in the same book, he wrote, "Countless studies have found that social relationships are the best guarantee of heightened well-being and lowered stress, both an antidote for depression and a prescription for high performance."

Surveys, be they informal or formal, are more than a diagnostic tool. They're a way to strengthen your relationship with your team. By listening and responding, you show that their voices matter, and that builds engagement from the ground up.

ANALYSING AND ACTING ON FEEDBACK

Let's talk about feedback, not just giving it but receiving and acting on it. When your team feels safe to share their thoughts and sees their input leading to real change, they'll trust you more and invest more deeply in their work. Maya Angelou's wisdom resonates deeply here: "If you don't like something, change it. If you can't change it, change your attitude." Her words highlight the transformative power of acting on feedback to bring about positive change.

Once you have feedback, don't let it gather dust. Prioritise the key themes and develop an action plan. Keep your team informed about what's being implemented and why. This transparency reinforces trust and demonstrates that their input drives decisions.

> The Ritz-Carlton's famous employee feedback system is a case in point. Daily "lineup" meetings allow employees to voice ideas, leading to immediate improvements in customer service *(Ritz-Carlton, 2020)*.

Perhaps you shudder at the thought of formal "lineup" meetings, but there are equally effective informal ways of encouraging employees to voice their ideas. The important thing is that they are comfortable in voicing them, safe in the knowledge that they won't be penalised for having done so. I guess I'm suggesting something similar to the foot soldier's question to an officer: "Permission to speak freely, Sir?"

Celebrate successes and acknowledge the impact of employee input. When team members see their feedback leading to meaningful improvements, they feel empowered to continue contributing ideas. This cycle of feedback and action creates a dynamic of trust, collaboration, and continuous improvement, propelling your team and organisation toward greater success.

POINTS TO PONDER

Engagement

How do we know when, and to what extent, people are engaged? Here are a few things to consider:

- How many unsolicited peer shout-outs are happening?

- The percentage of projects (however minor) that are at the suggestion of and/or driven by team members below management level.

- The frequency of informal social gatherings.

Treat KPIs as more than just numbers. See them as critical tools in measuring the quality of relationships within the matrix of a department and the organisation as a whole. You may not be able to come up with dry numbers, but what if you were to skip the 1–10 scale and instead colour-code them according to their quality as you see it? For example, blue indicates good performance, green signifies outstanding performance, yellow indicates a need for improvement, purple shows a breakdown, and finally, red indicates non-existent performance. Compare what colour others see as representing those relationships. There lies a basis for discussion if ever there was one.

To maximise the honesty and therefore value of the feedback, if your organisation permits, go for the casual conversation approach. You might want answers to the questions listed below, but you will get far better feedback if you allow the answers from some of them to emerge in conversation rather than asking them directly.

- As you see it, what do you think our mission is, and how do you see yourself fitting into it?

- What would help you feel more connected?

- What do you like, or even love, about your job?

- If you had a magic wand, what would you change?

You'll get more insight in a fifteen-minute conversation than in fifteen pages of cold data.

I know I'm all for the softly-softly, subtle approach (I call it stealth management), but this can go too far. Trust your gut is all very well, but experience and instinct need to be balanced with the kind of cold, hard facts that data gathering presents. For example, if the soft and cuddly KPIs show that happiness is rife within a department, and the support each member enjoys from their colleagues is applauded by all, but the easily measured productivity and efficiency have fallen off a cliff, then changes need to be made.

Risk

Strategic decisions often involve uncertainty. Reframe risk as an opportunity for growth, but make sure that you define the organisation's risk appetite. Provide clarity on what kinds of things are acceptable and what boundaries should not be breached. I agree that this can be highly complex. The degree of risk a senior manager might take may be far higher than that of a junior employee. But think of it in the financial terms of a company buyer's sign-off limit – the impact of your decision if it goes wrong cannot cost the organisation more than XXX.

Decision-Making

Encourage debate on past and possible future decisions. What is the impact, not only for the short term, but also in terms of long-term legacy?

Develop a decision-making framework. Effective decisions are rooted in clarity and structure. Take the time (which may be substantial, but will be worth it) to design a framework that spells out who can make which decisions, in what situations, and with whom they should collaborate. Most importantly, make sure everyone knows that if they are in doubt, they should default to following this framework. Like most practices aimed at long-term success, whatever you put in place should first be tested on a small scale and then refined as it's rolled out.

Follow Through

However, after that discussion, action must follow. What are employees themselves going to do to improve those pathways? And just as importantly, what are *you* going to do?

Consider hosting "You said - we did" sessions. They need not be formal affairs, so long as the message gets across. Here's what you told us, here's what we're trying to do about it, and here's where we still need ideas. You'll notice that the preceding sentence was expressed in the present tense. Some simple things can be quickly addressed, but others will take more time. Don't leave your team to assume that you have ignored their suggestions; involve them!

Chapter 9

Sustaining Employee Engagement

CREATING A CONTINUOUS IMPROVEMENT CULTURE

Question! What does a garden flower have in common with business? Answer! They are both trying to grow. Neither thrives by chance; both need ongoing care and attention. Creating a culture of continuous improvement is much the same. It's about fostering an environment where growth is constant and every team member feels empowered and valued to contribute to the organisation's evolution.

Albert Einstein told us: "Once you stop learning, you start dying." Continuous learning and improvement are the lifeblood of a thriving business and a motivated team. Start by encouraging a growth mindset within your team. Celebrate not just the successes but also the lessons learned from challenges. Show your team that mistakes are opportunities for growth, not failures to be feared. They need to know that it's okay to fail. I know I have said this before, but it bears repeating: when a team member was dismayed that they had made a mistake, my favourite saying was (and still is), "If this is going to be the worst mistake you make this year, I can live with that." It might have cost me a good deal of money, but the nature of business is to take risks. Sometimes they work out, and sometimes they don't. The point is that the team member already felt bad enough. There was no merit in making them feel worse. They would probably never want to make a decision again! If they were forced to make a decision, it would be made under stress and fear of failure, and when fear and stress walk through the door, the ability to make sensible, creative decisions jumps out of the window.

Provide tools and opportunities for development. Whether it's through training sessions, mentorship programmes, or access to industry resources, showing your commitment to their growth reinforces the idea that their future matters to you. Open communication plays a critical role. Regularly seek input from your team on processes, goals, and areas for improvement. Actively listen to their ideas and incorporate their feedback into your strategies. When your team sees that their suggestions lead to meaningful change, they're motivated to continue contributing.

Continuous improvement is a journey, not a destination. By fostering a culture that embraces growth, you create a workplace where engagement thrives and innovation flourishes.

ADAPTING TO CHANGE AND CHALLENGES

Change is inevitable, but how your team navigates it can make all the difference. As a leader, your role is to guide your team through challenges with confidence and clarity, showing them that adaptability is a strength. Throughout evolution, the creatures that were the most adaptable flourished. Those that were the least adaptable died out. John F. Kennedy wisely noted, "Change is the law of life. And those who look only to the past or present are certain to miss the future." Thriving amidst change requires leaders to look ahead and empower their teams to do the same. Start by being transparent about changes. Whether it's a shift in strategy, new goals, or external challenges, keep your team informed.

> Research by McKinsey & Company found that employees are five times more likely to remain engaged during periods of change when they understand the reasons behind it (*McKinsey, 2017*).

When people understand the "why," they're more likely to get on board. Encourage flexibility by modelling it yourself. Simply put, how can you expect others to show flexibility if you don't? Show your team that change isn't something to fear but an opportunity to innovate. Frame challenges as problems to solve together and invite their input on how to adapt. It's critical that you don't just pay lip service to this kind of thing, truly listen and act upon their input, and if you don't, or can't, tell them the reasons why. Then, and this is important too, give them a chance to respond to those reasons. It may well be that there is a misunderstanding on your part. Unless you explore it, you'll never know. This collaborative approach builds resilience and reinforces the idea that you're in it together.

Times of transition and change don't just bring extra stress to the boss's desk. Everyone feels it to varying degrees, and some can cope with it better than others. Provide extra support during transitions. Check in with your team regularly to address concerns and offer guidance. Equip them with the resources they need to succeed in the new landscape, whether that's additional training or simply a listening (and, so importantly, a caring) ear. Adapting to change is a skill that can be developed, and every challenge is an opportunity to strengthen it. By fostering a culture of adaptability, you prepare your team to face the future, replacing fear and stress with confidence and creativity.

CELEBRATING LONG-TERM SUCCESS

Let's take a moment to imagine the future. Your business has grown, your team is thriving, and you've achieved milestones that once seemed out of reach. How do you celebrate these moments? Recognising long-term success isn't just about looking back, but about building momentum for what's next.

Ralph Waldo Emerson said, "It's not the destination; it's the journey." Celebrating the journey reinforces the value of the path your team has taken together, highlighting the growth, resilience, and commitment that have led to success. Have fireside chats of your own. Start by reflecting on the journey. Share stories of the challenges you've overcome together and the victories you've achieved. These stories remind your team of how far they've come and reinforce their connection to the business's mission. Celebrate in ways that resonate with your team. Whether it's a team retreat, a simple thank-you speech, personalised tokens of appreciation, or, as I just mentioned, a fireside chat, the key is to make it meaningful and genuine.

Use these celebrations as an opportunity to refocus on the future. Highlight new goals and the role each team member will play in achieving them. First as you see it and then as they see it. Don't impose a goal; collaborate with them on forming one that they can buy into. This forward-looking approach keeps the momentum going and ensures that success is a stepping stone, not a finish line.

Celebrating long-term success is about more than recognition; it's about building a culture of appreciation and motivation that sustains engagement for years to come. If you can succeed in helping them to be proud to be part of it, together, you and your team can achieve incredible things.

POINTS TO PONDER

A Variant on the Suggestion Box

I want to touch on the good old-fashioned suggestion box. Back in the day (whenever that was), suggestion boxes would be strategically placed around businesses, inviting suggestions on slips of paper. They could be anonymous, which probably invited a fair few less-than-complimentary notes. Old hat they may be, but on occasions they would come up with a gem. They offered anonymity, which is difficult to replicate in the days of emails and social media. Without anonymity, suggestions that might be world-beaters would never see the light of day. So what's the solution? Make an anonymous channel available so that team members will not fear being ridiculed. Ask anyone who contributes to place a password on their suggestion. If it is adopted or taken seriously, they can be rewarded for it or involved in the project needed to bring it to fruition. However, and it's quite a big however, wouldn't it be better to create an atmosphere where everyone is comfortable putting their ideas forward?

Create a "Lessons Learned, Lessons Lived" shared space for people to browse, contribute to, and discuss suggestions that have been put forward. This normalises learning, reduces fear of failure, and builds a collective wisdom bank. Of the ones that have been acted upon, open up conversations on:

- A mistake that turned into growth.

- A "what we'd do differently" reflection.

- A surprising win and how it unfolded.

Uncertainty and Change

There is not a business or organisation on the planet that has not had to go through change and uncertainty. It could be due to growth, a decline in sales, a side swipe resulting from a change in legislation, or a myriad of other reasons. Change is uncomfortable, but it is almost always an opportunity to grow, forcing us to develop our resilience. Some can cope with the stress of change and uncertainty better than others, but everyone should be given a chance to contribute to navigating through such times.

When facing change or uncertainty, consider either holding 15-minute team "resilience rounds" or engaging in one-on-one conversations. Use three simple prompts:

- What's changing?

- What are we unsure about?

- What strengths can we draw on?

Make it brief, make it honest, and make sure you go first. Modelling vulnerability in uncertain times creates safety for others to open up too.

The Power of Laughter

Laughter is a double-edged sword. If we can laugh in certain situations, or at ourselves, it can bring huge benefits, but it can also be destructive. If a team member is laughed at and ridiculed for a suggestion or idea, their future creativity will take a severe hit; it may even be killed off forever.. It might be ideal, but it's certainly not practical to insist on a no-laughter policy when evaluating new ideas. Stifled laughter or sniggering is equally destructive. What's the answer? Tell stories of when a suggestion was laughed at but went on to become a complete winner. If you like, try to gamify it along the lines of, if you don't raise a laugh, you're not trying. Put yourself out there to be laughed at. Let it be known that those who provoke the most mirth are the winners in this game.

You might want to create an award for the daft idea of the month, and when it's presented, make a point of the fact that without so-called daft ideas, history shows that very little progress would have been made. There would still be square wheels and no sliced bread! Make the daft idea contributor a hero. You might even want to consider gamifying the whole process in a light-hearted competition:

- Worst-sounding idea with the best potential upside

- Funniest suggestion that might just work

The dafter the better, but the reward has a twist: the winner gets to pitch the idea seriously at the next strategy meeting. Laughter + legitimacy = innovation unlocked.

Don't Forget to Celebrate

When it comes to celebrating success, encourage the lateral flow of gratitude and congratulations. Such things delivered from the c-suite are all very well, but their impact pales into insignificance compared to when they come from a workmate or colleague in another part of the business who appreciates what you have done.

Engaging team members in conversations in times of uncertainty and change is all very well, but it's too easy to forget them when times are good and the business is flying. Your team is part of that, too. Don't be some kind of diva and take all of the plaudits yourself, leaving them in the shadows. Bring them out onto the metaphorical stage so that they, too, can enjoy the plaudits of success. Celebrate with them. And it's not just about big wins, build a "Celebrate the Climb Wall."

Instead of just showcasing big wins, create a visual timeline of smaller progress steps. Include things like:

- What hurdles did we overcome this quarter?

- What micro-successes added up to the big one?

Use stories, sticky notes, or team shout-outs. This reminds everyone: the journey is the achievement.

On the subject of celebration, make a point of recognising achievements and milestones such as long tenures, upskilling, or completion of a project or task. This is where I set aside my reluctance to take the formal route. On these occasions, formal recognition may be the best approach. Create certificates, personalised awards, or use simple speeches. Marking progress with a ceremony shows your team that time and effort matter.

Everyone Is Entitled to Their Own Journey

Encourage people to be open with their goals and ambitions. Some will align with the business, others won't, but that's fine. Help them to grow towards their goals.

Ask questions such as:

- Where do you want to be in three years?

- What would help you most right now?

Let them know that whatever their reply, you won't hold it against them. If you've already nurtured the kind of relationship we have talked about in this fireside chat, there is a good chance they'll believe you. If they stay, they will be a great asset. If they grow, let them fly. What you have lost in an employee, you'll have gained in an ambassador for the business out there in the world.

Challenge your team to take time to discover courses or programmes they might like to participate in, or that others within the organisation might like. If finances permit, let them enrol. If finances are tight, make it a joint goal between them and the business.

I hope that these points to ponder honour the truth that engagement doesn't come from motivational posters or KPIs alone. It's about love, laughter, learning, and leadership that's deeply human.

Chapter 10

Inspiring the Future

THE EVOLUTION OF TEAM ENGAGEMENT

As our fire sinks to its glowing embers, let's wrap things up and reflect on how far you've come. The way businesses think about team engagement has evolved. It's no longer just about productivity or output, but about creating an environment where people feel connected, valued, and inspired. Engagement today is about cultivating a shared purpose that transforms work into something meaningful.

Margaret Wheatley captured this sentiment perfectly: "There is no power for change greater than a community discovering what it cares about." The essence of team engagement lies in building a connected and motivated community that works together toward shared goals. Let's start with the foundation: connection. When your team feels truly connected to one another, to you, and to the business's mission, they become unstoppable. Connection isn't just built through meetings or memos. Indeed, used in isolation, they can even be counterproductive. Connection is fostered through trust, open communication, and shared experiences.

If you need convincing of the merits of what I am saying, perhaps this will help: Research from Gallup found that highly engaged teams exhibit 59% lower turnover and 41% lower absenteeism (*Gallup, 2017*).

Engagement also thrives when employees see how their work contributes to the bigger picture. It encourages them, at least to some extent, to see things through the boss's eyes; maybe even think like the boss. Above all else, this is the way to end isolation and, yes, I'll say it, the loneliness that goes with being the boss. Leadership is the engine of engagement. As a leader, your actions, words, and energy set the tone. When you show enthusiasm for the mission, your team will follow. When you demonstrate care and respect for each individual, they'll feel valued. And when you invest in their growth, they'll invest in the business.

LEADING WITH PURPOSE

What drives you? What gets you out of bed every morning, ready to face the challenges of running a business? That sense of purpose isn't just for you; it's the spark that can ignite your team. Leading with purpose means sharing your vision and making it something your team can rally around.

Maya Angelou's words kind of say it all here: "Nothing will work unless you do." Living your vision daily and actively engaging in the mission you lead sets a powerful example for your team. Start by articulating your why. Why does your business exist? What impact do you want it to have on your customers, your community, and the world? Share this vision openly and often. When your team understands the purpose behind their work, it gives them something to believe in and work toward.

> Simon Sinek's principle of starting with *why* has been applied successfully by companies like Apple, whose mission-driven leadership has inspired employees and customers alike (*Sinek, 2009*).

Purpose-driven leadership also means walking the walk. If collaboration is part of your vision, model it in your daily interactions. If innovation is a cornerstone of your purpose, celebrate creative thinking and risk-taking. When your actions align with your words, you build trust and inspire your team to follow your example.

Remember, purpose isn't static. As your business grows, your vision may evolve. Bring your team along for the journey, involving them in shaping the future. This shared ownership strengthens their connection to the business and keeps the fire of engagement burning bright.

THE POWER OF MENTORING

Let's talk about mentoring. It's something that can have a profound impact, not just on organisational growth, but also on personal growth. It can extend far beyond knowledge and skills transfer. It builds friendships and strong connections. It empowers individuals and cultivates a culture of continuous development.

Mentoring isn't a one-way street. Both mentor and mentee have much to gain. Mentors can gain fresh perspectives that might otherwise pass them by. It's all about active listening by both sides.

At this point, I should add a caveat. As beneficial as mentoring can be, in the wrong hands, it can be destructive. The last thing any organisation needs is a bad apple being chosen to mentor someone; their jaundiced opinions and attitude will spread like a virus. And here's something else to consider: if that kind of attitude is the reason why you would not want a particular person to be a mentor, should they not be working in some other organisation?

That said, I can't overemphasise how mentoring has the potential to bring a team together in ways you might never have thought possible until you witness the results: a closely bonded team, all pulling in the same direction.

Mentoring isn't something to operate vertically from superior down to subordinate. It should be used horizontally among people of the same rank and across departments, helping create the kind of trust, connections, understanding, and empathy that constitute the glue that bonds an organisation.

I'm a lover of informality, and in that regard, spontaneous mentoring is a wonderful thing. But this is one of those occasions when informal meetups might not be enough. It's important to set structured programs in place. They should be such that everyone buys into them and the benefits that mentoring brings. Remember, it starts with you. Who in your team can you learn something from? And don't say "No one."

I've already said how mentoring can bring a team together, but there is an added bonus. A mentorship program will help identify and nurture future leaders. You should make that identification a dynamic process. Someone who at first looks ordinary might blossom into a star as they grow in confidence. As if that's not enough, there's a second bonus: Future leaders might emerge not just from the ranks of the mentees but also from among the mentors who might find new enthusiasm and drive when asked to take on the role.

CREATING A LEGACY OF MOTIVATION

Now, let's think about the long term. What kind of legacy do you want to leave as a leader? Building a motivated team isn't just about hitting targets today; it's about creating a culture that endures, one where people feel empowered and inspired long after you've moved on to your next challenge.

Warren Bennis put it beautifully: "Leadership is the capacity to translate vision into reality." The legacy of a leader lies in converting their values and vision into a culture that outlasts their tenure. A legacy of motivation starts with your values. Infuse them into every aspect of the business, from how you hire to how you celebrate success. When values are lived, not just spoken, they become the foundation of a thriving culture.

> Ben & Jerry's has embedded social justice into its mission, creating a workplace where employees feel they are contributing to a greater cause (*Ben & Jerry's, 2021*).

Invest in your team's growth. Provide opportunities for learning, mentorship, and leadership development. Show your team that you're as committed to their futures as you are to the business's success.

> Research by LinkedIn Learning shows that companies that invest in employee development see 94% higher retention rates (*LinkedIn Learning, 2021*).

Celebrate the journey, not just the milestones. Acknowledge the effort and dedication your team brings every day. Build traditions that reinforce the culture you've created, whether it's an annual retreat, monthly shout-outs, or simply taking the time to say, "thank you."

Your legacy isn't just about what you achieve; it's about how you make others feel. By fostering a culture of motivation, connection, and purpose, you'll leave behind something far greater than a successful business. You'll leave behind a team that's ready to carry the mission forward, inspired and capable of achieving even more.

As we sit here together, imagining what's next, I hope you feel a renewed sense of excitement. Your leadership has the power to transform not just your business but the lives of the people who make it thrive. Let's keep building something incredible, one purposeful step at a time. And remember this: "'People will forget what you said, people will forget what you did, but people will never forget how you made them feel." — Maya Angelou.

POINTS TO PONDER

Think in terms of legacy. What do you want to leave behind when you're no longer there? Be sure to share that with the entire team. Encourage them to do the same. Let me give you an example: When a department manager sees what you have done, she declares that her goal is to create a department that can run smoothly without her. She will train and mentor people to be as skilled as she is in her job, enabling them to step into her shoes. Her legacy will be that she leaves the department in a better state than when she first took on the job. But it's not just about managers; a production worker can declare that they want to leave a legacy by training and mentoring others to instantly replace them when they are gone. Recognise and reward them for the legacy they are creating. Make it known that the very best are those who are willing to train others to take their place, but make sure that those "replacements" are not allowed to accelerate the process. If it happens once, it will kill the legacy building process stone dead. Turkeys don't vote for Christmas.

Don't just rely on spontaneous and informal mentoring. Create a formal, structured program that runs through every level of the organisation. Encourage everyone to buy into the idea by highlighting how mentors can gain every bit as much as mentees. Make recognition of mentoring a key part of the recognition and gratitude matrix.

Create an environment where people feel connected. They feel that they matter and are inspired to be part of your collective future. Do that by leading from the front. Engage in the programs you are asking them to go through. Listen wholeheartedly with two ears; in other words, show you care. Think of it as a cascade, a champagne fountain. You pour your empathy and care into the top, and it flows down and around throughout the organisation.

How will you know when it is working? Try these answers for starters:

- When junior members of your team are not afraid to approach you with an idea or a suggestion.

- When you hear that employees have been singing the company's praises when they are outside of the work environment.

- When you see examples of team members voluntarily helping each other.

- When you never again hear the phrase, "It's not MY job to do that."

- When you notice that social gatherings are taking place amongst team members.

- When they invite YOU.

The challenge is to become the kind of leader who doesn't just want to win, but to uplift, inspire, and leave something better than they found it.

Author's Closing Comments

I didn't set out to write this book as some voluminous tome, and in that regard, I have succeeded, as it only runs to a few pages. I certainly didn't write it to gather dust in the darkest corner of obscure libraries. It is simply a series of thoughts and ideas presented in the form of a fireside chat. I hope that within its pages you will discover, or perhaps rediscover, a few ideas that might help you build something special. Something you can be proud of, and even a source of joy. I wish you well.

Feel free to reach out to me at *info@thelonelyseat.com*

Bibliography

Achor, S. (2010). *The Happiness Advantage: The Seven Principles of Positive Psychology That Fuel Success and Performance at Work.* New York: Crown Business.

Adobe. (2018) *The Benefits of Continuous Feedback.* [Online]. Available at: https://www.adobe.com/creativecloud/design/discover/continuous-feedback.html (Accessed: 19 August 2025).

Angelou, M. (1993). *Family Circle interview with Maya Angelou.* [Online]. Family Circle, 19 January. Available at: https://www.familycircle.com (Accessed: 19 August 2025). *(Quote "People will forget what you said…" widely attributed, but not verbatim, in her published works.)*

Angelou, M. (n.d.) *"If you don't like something, change it. If you can't change it, change your attitude."* [Online]. Available at: https://www.goodreads.com/quotes/3812 (Accessed: 19 August 2025).

Angelou, M. (n.d.) *"Nothing will work unless you do."* [Online]. Available at: https://www.goodreads.com/quotes/963-nothing-will-work-unless-you-do (Accessed: 19 August 2025).

AT&T. (2018) *Building Leadership Through Mentorship.* [Online]. Available at: https://about.att.com/story/2018/leadership_mentorship.html (Accessed: 19 August 2025).

Ben & Jerry's. (2021) *Values-Led Leadership at Ben & Jerry's.* [Online]. Available at: https://www.benjerry.com (Accessed: 19 August 2025).

Bennis, W. (1985). *Leaders: Strategies for Taking Charge.* New York: Harper & Row.

Blanchard, K. (2009). *"Feedback is the breakfast of champions."* [Online]. Available at: https://www.kenblanchardbooks.com/feedback-is-the-breakfast-of-champions (Accessed: 19 August 2025). *(Original phrase credited* *to Rick Tate.)*

Bock, L. (2015). *Work Rules!: Insights from Inside Google that Will Transform How You Live and Lead.* New York: Twelve.

Buffett, W. (1994) *Berkshire Hathaway Shareholder Letter 1994.* [Online]. Available at: https://www.berkshirehathaway.com/letters/1994.html (Accessed: 19 August 2025).

Carnegie, D. (1936). *How to Win Friends and Influence People.* New York: Simon & Schuster.

CLC. (2020) *The Impact of Constructive Feedback on Performance.* [Online]. Available at: https://www.clc.com (Accessed: 19 August 2025).

Covey, S.R. (1989). *The 7 Habits of Highly Effective People.* New York: Free Press.

Darwin, C. (1859). *On the Origin of Species by Means of Natural Selection.* London: John Murray.

Drucker, P.F. (1999). *Management Challenges for the 21st Century.* New York: Harper Business.

Drucker, P.F. (n.d.) *"The most serious mistakes are not being made as a result of wrong answers..."* [Online]. Paraphrased in *The Effective Executive* (1967) and *The Practice of Management* (1954). Available at: https://www.goodreads.com/quotes/179663 (Accessed: 19 August 2025).

Drucker, P.F. (n.d.) *"The most important thing in communication..."* [Online]. Frequently attributed, but not in Drucker's published works. Available at: https://www.oxfordreference.com/view/10.1093/acref/9780191826719.001. 0001/q-oro-ed4-00012211 (Accessed: 19 August 2025).

Drucker, P.F. (n.d.) *"What gets measured gets managed."* [Online]. Commonly attributed to Drucker, but no evidence in his published works. Closest verifiable use: Kaplan, R.S. and Norton, D.P. (1992). Available at:

https://hbr.org/1992/01/the-balanced-scorecard-measures-that-drive-performance (Accessed: 19 August 2025).

Einstein, A. (n.d.) *"Once you stop learning, you start dying."* [Online]. Available at: https://www.goodreads.com/quotes/18896 (Accessed: 19 August 2025).

Emerson, R.W. (n.d.) *"It's not the destination, it's the journey."* [Online]. Available at: https://quoteinvestigator.com/2012/08/31/life-journey/ (Accessed: 19 August 2025).

Franklin, B. (n.d.) *"Without continual growth and progress..."* [Online]. Available at: https://www.brainyquote.com (Accessed: 19 August 2025).

Frost & Sullivan. (2021) *The Benefits of Unified Communication Tools.* [Online]. Available at: https://www.frost.com (Accessed: 19 August 2025).

Gallup. (2017) *State of the Global Workplace.* [Online]. Available at: https://www.gallup.com/workplace/238079/state-global-workplace-2017.aspx (Accessed: 19 August 2025).

Goleman, D. (1995). *Emotional Intelligence: Why It Can Matter More Than IQ.* New York: Bantam Books.

Hemingway, E. (n.d.) *"The best way to find out if you can trust somebody is to trust them."* [Online]. Closest variant in *Selected Letters 1917–1961.* Available at: https://www.goodreads.com/quotes/185425 (Accessed: 19 August 2025).

Hsieh, T. (2010). *Delivering Happiness: A Path to Profits, Passion, and Purpose.* New York: Grand Central Publishing.

HubSpot. (2019) *The HubSpot Culture Code.* [Online]. Available at: https://www.hubspot.com/company/culture (Accessed: 19 August 2025).

International Coaching Federation (ICF). (2019) *The Impact of Coaching on Business Performance.* [Online]. Available at: https://coachingfederation.org/research (Accessed: 19 August 2025).

Kaplan, R.S. and Norton, D.P. (1992) 'The balanced scorecard: Measures that drive performance', *Harvard Business Review*, 70(1), pp. 71–79.

Keller, H. (1903). *Optimism: An Essay.* London: Crowell. *(Quote paraphrased as: "The only thing worse than being blind is having sight but no vision.")*

Kennedy, J.F. (1963) *Speech at the Assembly Hall of the Paulskirche, Frankfurt, Federal Republic of Germany, 25 June 1963.* Washington, DC: John F. Kennedy Presidential Library and Museum. [Online]. Available at: https://www.jfklibrary.org/archives/other-resources/john-f-kennedy-speeches/frankfurt-west-germany-19630625 (Accessed: 19 August 2025).

Lewis, C.S. (n.d.) *"Integrity is doing the right thing, even when no one is watching."* [Online]. Misattributed; originates from: Marshall, C. (2003). *Shattering the Glass Slipper.* Jackson, MS: The Encouragement Group, Inc., p. 142. Available at: https://www.goodreads.com/quotes/43090 (Accessed: 19 August 2025).

LinkedIn Learning. (2021) *Workplace Learning Report.* [Online]. Available at: https://learning.linkedin.com/resources/workplace-learning-report (Accessed: 19 August 2025).

Marshall, C. (2003). *Shattering the Glass Slipper.* Jackson, MS: The Encouragement Group, Inc., p. 142.

McKinsey & Company. (2017) *The Role of Transparency in Employee Engagement.* [Online]. Available at: https://www.mckinsey.com/business-functions/organization/our-insights/the-role-of-transparency-in-employee-engagement (Accessed: 19 August 2025).

McKinsey & Company. (2017) *The Value of Communication in Reducing Turnover.* [Online]. Available at: https://www.mckinsey.com (Accessed: 19 August 2025).

Megginson, L.C. (1963) 'Lessons from Europe for American Business', *Southwestern Social Science Quarterly*, 44(1), pp. 3–13.

Microsoft. (2020) *How Satya Nadella Transformed Microsoft's Culture.* [Online]. Available at: https://news.microsoft.com/stories/satya-nadella/ (Accessed: 19 August 2025).

Mulally, A. (n.d.) *"The customer is the most important part of the assembly line."* [Online]. Available at: https://www.goodreads.com/quotes/1011076 (Accessed: 19 August 2025).

Netflix. (2020) *The Power of Trust: How Netflix Leads.* [Online]. Available at: https://www.netflix.com (Accessed: 19 August 2025).

Patagonia. (2020) *Our Commitment to Activism.* [Online]. Available at: https://www.patagonia.com (Accessed: 19 August 2025).

Peters, T.J. and Waterman, R.H. (1982). *In Search of Excellence: Lessons from America's Best-Run Companies.* New York: Harper & Row.

PwC. (2018) *The Trust Edge: How Trust Impacts Productivity.* [Online]. Available at: https://www.pwc.com (Accessed: 19 August 2025).

Ritz-Carlton. (2020) *The Power of Daily Feedback.* [Online]. Available at: https://www.ritzcarlton.com/leadership/daily-feedback (Accessed: 19 August 2025).

Salesforce. (2020) *Circle of Success: Celebrating Team Achievements.* [Online]. Available at: https://www.salesforce.com/resources/articles/circle-of-success/ (Accessed: 19 August 2025).

Salesforce. (2020) *Salesforce Careers: Employee Recognition.* [Online]. Available at: https://www.salesforce.com (Accessed: 19 August 2025).

Schultz, H. (2011). *Onward: How Starbucks Fought for Its Life Without Losing Its Soul.* Emmaus, PA: Rodale Books.

Shopify. (2020) *How We Hire at Shopify.* [Online]. Available at: https://www.shopify.com/careers/how-we-hire (Accessed: 19 August 2025).

SHRM (Society for Human Resource Management). (2020) *The Value of*

Employee Surveys. [Online]. Available at:
https://www.shrm.org/resourcesandtools/hr-topics/organizational-and-employee-development/pages/employee-surveys.aspx (Accessed: 19 August 2025).

Sinek, S. (2009) *Start With Why: How Great Leaders Inspire Everyone to Take Action.* London: Penguin.

Slack. (2020) *How Slack Transforms Communication for Global Teams.* [Online]. Available at: https://www.slack.com (Accessed: 19 August 2025).

Wheatley, M.J. (2002). *Turning to One Another: Simple Conversations to Restore Hope to the Future.* San Francisco: Berrett-Koehler.